SpringerBriefs in Geography

SpringerBriefs in Geography presents concise summaries of cutting-edge research and practical applications across the fields of physical, environmental and human geography. It publishes compact refereed monographs under the editorial supervision of an international advisory board with the aim to publish 8 to 12 weeks after acceptance. Volumes are compact, 50 to 125 pages, with a clear focus. The series covers a range of content from professional to academic such as: timely reports of state-of-the art analytical techniques, bridges between new research results, snapshots of hot and/or emerging topics, elaborated thesis, literature reviews, and in-depth case studies.

The scope of the series spans the entire field of geography, with a view to significantly advance research. The character of the series is international and multidisciplinary and will include research areas such as: GIS/cartography, remote sensing, geographical education, geospatial analysis, techniques and modeling, landscape/regional and urban planning, economic geography, housing and the built environment, and quantitative geography. Volumes in this series may analyze past, present and/or future trends, as well as their determinants and consequences. Both solicited and unsolicited manuscripts are considered for publication in this series.

SpringerBriefs in Geography will be of interest to a wide range of individuals with interests in physical, environmental and human geography as well as for researchers from allied disciplines.

More information about this series at http://www.springer.com/series/10050

Melanie Fasche

Making Value and Career Building in the Creative Economy

Evidence from Contemporary Visual Art

Springer

Melanie Fasche
Independent Scholar
Toronto
Canada

ISSN 2211-4165 ISSN 2211-4173 (electronic)
SpringerBriefs in Geography
ISBN 978-3-319-54029-0 ISBN 978-3-319-54030-6 (eBook)
DOI 10.1007/978-3-319-54030-6

Library of Congress Control Number: 2017933550

Printed on acid-free paper

This Springer imprint is published by Springer Nature
The registered company is Springer International Publishing AG
The registered company address is: Gewerbestrasse 11, 6330 Cham, Switzerland

Acknowledgements

This research was greatly supported in multiple ways by supervisors, peers, senior scholars, friends, and family, as well as a range of institutions. All this support was crucial for a flexible and rather independent way of working immersed in a location known for its creative scenes away from an institutional environment.

My sincerest thank you and appreciation to Gernot Grabher for supervising this work. I am very grateful for all his constructive criticism, our discussions, and his advice. I am also very thankful to Gerhard O. Braun for co-supervising this work. His critical questions and helpful comments are gratefully acknowledged.

I would like to thank the following senior scholars and peers for interesting conversations and helpful comments on working papers and drafts. Many thanks to Michaël Deinema, David Halle, Andrew Harris, Meric Gertler, Iain Hay, Johan Jansson, Jennifer Kondo, Jenny Sjöholm, Kevin Stolarick, and Elisabeth Tiso.

I am also grateful to senior scholars, peers, friends, and family for inspiring conversations about this work, helpful comments on presentations, or accompanying me with their friendship and love. Many thanks to Till Brühhöfener-McCourt, Roberta Comunian, Johannes Glückler, Joachim Griess, Marietta Hoferer, Brian J. Hracs, Oliver Ibert, Wolfgang Jager, Petra Jähnke, Katja Jahn, Doreen Jakob, Erik Jäckel, Wolfgang Jager, Heike Jezewski, Heiderose Kilper, Kerstin Kloppe, Bodo Kubartz, Bastian Lange, Jochen Langenberger, Bettina Lelong, Elizabeth Mack, Kate McCourt, Stewart McSherry, Marco Mundelius, Paul Nagle, Deike Peters, Josephine Rekers, Ingo Röhle, Godela Rossner, Michael Salber, Wendy Sarkissian, Stefan Schmitt, Gregory Sholette, Volker Spelthann, Susanne Sporrer, Rüdiger Ulrich, Tina Wentrup, Alexandra Wittek, Bruni Zinner, and Dietmar Zinner.

A very special thank you to my closest friend Doreen Eichler for her support throughout the journey of this work, and all our conversations about and around this research.

I would like to thank the following people and institutions for supporting me with opportunities necessary to pursue this work, such as conducting fieldwork overseas, presenting and discussing my work in progress, meeting and engaging with peers and other researchers, and learning about different themes and perspectives. Many thanks to Gerhard O. Braun and Katja Sussner on behalf of the Center for Metropolitan Studies (CMS) at Technical University Berlin in cooperation with Volker Berghahn on behalf of Columbia University; Jenny Sjöholm on behalf of the Department of Social and Economic Geography at Uppsala University; David Halle on behalf of the Department of Sociology at UCLA; Macro Mundelius on behalf of the German Institute for Economic Research (DIW); Oli Mould and Allen Watson on behalf of the Globalization and World Cities Research Network at Loughborough University; Gernot Grabher and Hugues Jeannerat on behalf of Urban and Regional Economic Studies at HafenCity University Hamburg; Heiderose Kilper and Ulf Matthiesen on behalf of the Institute for Regional Development and Structural Planning (IRS); Brian J. Hracs, Doreen Jakob, Karen M. King, Dieter Kogler, and Kevin Stolarick on behalf of the Martin Prosperity Institute at the Joseph L. Rotman School of Management at the University of Toronto; Georg Schreyögg on behalf of the Path Dependency Research Center at the School of Business and Economics at Free University Berlin; Caroline Chapain, Nick Clifton, and Roberta Comunian on behalf of the Regional Studies Association; Astrid Preuss and Jörn Weinhold on behalf of the Research School at HafenCity University Hamburg; John D. Graham, David B. Audretsch, and Michael Rushton on behalf of the School of Public and Environmental Affairs (SPEA) at Indiana University; Andrew Harris on behalf of the Urban Laboratory at University College London; and Ron Boschma on behalf of the International Ph.D. course in Economic Geography at the Faculty of Geosciences at Utrecht University.

Last but not least, I am particularly grateful to all the gallerists who took time for the interviews and provided insight in the first place.

Addendum: I would like to thank the three anonymous reviewers for sharing their perspectives and helping me to reflect on my work, and Stefan Einarson and his team at Springer for directing and guiding the publication process.

Contents

Author's Note

This work is a doctoral thesis defended in Urban and Regional Economic Studies at HafenCity University Hamburg, Germany. Minor revisions to the original manuscript titled "Making Value: Contemporary Visual Art, Careers and Place" were made for this publication.

Abstract

This work aims to reveal the organizational and geographical logics of making value and career building in the creative economy that lead to an unequal distribution of rewards among creative workers. Based on evidence from a case study of contemporary visual art, this work builds a heuristic conceptual framework, tentatively dubbed value-making ecology. Central to the conceptualization is the premise that creativity and talent are necessary but not sufficient conditions for enduring value of individual works and stable long-term careers, instead creativity and talent need to be valued to eventually be rewarded. It is argued that making value and career building is a competitive socially and spatially entangled process facilitated by a selection system of institutions and practices. Although the world of contemporary visual art is special in many ways, its key logics of making value and career building seem to be paradigmatic for the determination of economic value and competitive success in the wider creative economy.

Keywords Creative economy · Making value · Career building · Competition · Unequal rewards · Case study · Contemporary visual art · Selection system · Institutions · Practices

Chapter 1
Prologue

Abstract The *Prologue* outlines the main characteristics of the art market boom between the early 1990s and 2008. It highlights an unprecedented growth of the art world and sketches the growing distortion of price levels for living artists at auction and real values supported by career building by commercial gallerists symptomatic for over-speculation on enduring value during boom times.

Keywords Art market · Boom · Contemporary visual art · Gallerist · Auction · Speculation · Price · Value

Since the last big art market bust in the early 1990s the art world of contemporary visual art has witnessed an unprecedented growth. The number of artists, collectors and those mediating between supply and demand as well as the number of venues and events where artworks are shown to the public increased far and wide and expanded the art world well beyond its Western center (McCarthy et al. 2005: xvii). Volumes of sales soared and price levels for living artists at auction reached new historical heights. One million dollars became the new "ten grand" (Vogel 2007a).

Between July 1, 1991 and July 1, 2008 the price index for contemporary visual artworks at auction increased by 132% amounting for a growth rate almost five times higher than those in other auction segments such as Old Masters, 19th century, Modern and Postwar Art (Artprice 2008: 5). In November 2007 a new record for living artists at auction was set for Jeff Koons' "Hanging Heart (Magenta/Gold)" sold for a hammer price of US$23.5 million during the Fall Auctions at Sotheby's New York (Vogel 2007b). Only later it was revealed that the US-American superstar gallerist Larry Gagosian had bought the artwork on behalf of the Ukrainian billionaire Victor Pinchuk (Economist 2010) who represents a new generation of wealthy private collectors from places beyond the Western art world (Fasche 2013: 178). Likewise galleries reported a fast pace of doing business and frequently selling out both gallery shows and when participating in art fairs (Adam et al. 2007). The enormous liquidity in the art market and the amount of record prices at auction that were outperforming stocks fuelled the perception that

M. Fasche, *Making Value and Career Building in the Creative Economy*,
SpringerBriefs in Geography, DOI 10.1007/978-3-319-54030-6_1

contemporary visual art may be a promising alternative investment (Feigen 2007: 28; McCarthy et al. 2005: 67).

The booming art market prompted discussions about a speculative bubble and consequences of its likely bust. Art world insiders observed a growing distortion between price levels and real values for living artists at auction although the boom didn't affect all artists in the same manner. Even at the height of the boom only the artworks of a selected group of "1% of 1% of 1% of all artists" (Saltz 2009) had become very expensive whereas the price level for artworks of the majority of artists stayed flat or even declined (Pogrebin and Flynn 2011). There was general agreement in the art world that the over-speculation on enduring value and resale potential would sooner or later be stopped by an external shock (Feigen 2007: 28). Market believers, however, expected that increasingly globalizing demand would be able to compensate for a slump in demand in a recessionary West and soften a potential downturn—contrary to the last recession when demand had dried up completely (Feigen 2007: 28).

Although no one knew when and how the bubble would burst, the art world welcomed an end of market excesses and hoped for a renewed interest in art itself (Petterson 2008). The looming recession was seen as an opportunity for a return to critical reflection and dialogue about artworks facilitated by the art historical establishment of museums, alternative spaces, curators, critics and historians (Baer 2008; Kallir 2007), and thus be a chance for gallerists committed to building stable long-term art careers to regain a balance with auction houses in the market (Petterson 2008). It was anticipated that once liquidity vanished interest would shift from seemingly over-valued celebrity artists at auction towards new art from local up-and-coming talents represented by galleries (Petterson 2008). Hence, the art world recalled the emergence of the Young British Artists (YBAs) whose great success has largely been interpreted as a product of the last art market recession in the early 1990s (Ruiz and Pes 2010; Stallabrass 2006: 295).

In September 2008 an experimental auction sale at Sotheby's London not only became a record sale for a single artist at auction but also stretched the rules of the art market and became a landmark event in the history of the art market (Thornton 2008a). Damien Hirst, one of these YBAs back in the 1990s, dodged his gallerists who had been supporting and building his career for nearly 20 years and instead used the auction room as alternative channel of distribution for 200+ new artworks straight from his art studio (Bevan 2008; Thornton 2008b). Hirst's auction sale "Beautiful Inside My Head Forever" surpassed expectations with 218 of 223 lots being sold earning an exorbitant total of US$200 million (Sotheby's 2008)—causing unease among gallerists that other artists may follow suit (Bevan 2008; Thornton 2008b). The very same days Lehman Brothers, one of the largest American investment banks, had to file for bankruptcy—an external shock catalyzing the end of over-speculation on enduring value in the weeks and months following.

References

Adam, G., Gerlis, M., Dobrzynski, J., & Mason B. (2007, December 8–9). Art market alive and kicking. Dealers report strong sales despite fears of economic downturn. *The Art Newspaper*, 1.

Artprice. (2008). *Contemporary art market. The artprice annual report*. http://imgpublic.artprice.com/pdf/fiac08en.pdf. Accessed 8 February 2013.

Baer, J. (2008, October). Speculation in young artists is over, and the smaller dealers will be hurt the most. Perhaps the silver lining is a return to the importance of museums and critics. *The Art Newspaper, 195*.

Bevan, R. (2008, July–August). Damien Hirst is rewriting the rules of the market (1). *The Art Newspaper, 193*, 31.

Economist (2010, July 2). *The elephant in the room*. http://www.economist.com/blogs/newsbook/2010/07/artview. Accessed 8 February 2013.

Fasche, M. (2013). Making art history—Wealthy private collectors and contemporary visual art. In Hay, I. (Ed.), *Geographies of the super-rich* (pp. 171–185). London: Edward Elgar.

Feigen, R. (2007, July–August). It's definitely a bubble, but when it will burst is anybody's guess. *The Art Newspaper, 182*, 28.

Kallir, J. (2007, July–August). The problem with a collector-driven market. *The Art Newspaper, 182*, 29.

McCarthy, K. F., Ondaatje, E. H., Brooks, A., & Szántó, A. (2005). *A portrait of the visual arts. Meeting the challenges of a new era*. Santa Monica, CA: RAND Corporation.

Petterson, A. (2008, November). Tough times will provide opportunities. *The Art Newspaper, 196*.

Pogrebin, R., & Flynn, K. (2011, May 30). Does money grow on art market trees? Not for everyone. *The New York Times*. http://www.nytimes.com/2011/05/31/arts/design/not-all-art-market-prices-are-soaring.html?_r=0. Accessed June 2 2011.

Ruiz, C., & Pes, J. (2010, June 18–20). Still a "sensation"? How much do the Young British Artists matter as they enter middle age. *The Art Newspaper*, 2.

Saltz, J. (2009, February 18). The art market is more moral than the stock market. *The Art Newspaper*.

Sotheby's. (2008). *Auction results: Damien Hirst—Beautiful inside my head forever*. http://www.sothebys.com/en/auctions/2008/damien-hirst-beautiful-inside-my-head-forever.html. Accessed September 25 2008.

Stallabrass, J. (2006). *High art lite. The rise and fall of Young British Art*. (revised and expanded edition). London: Verso.

Thornton, S. (2008a). In and out of love with Damien Hirst. *The Art Newspaper, 195*, 39.

Thornton, S. (2008b, July–August). Damien Hirst is rewriting the rules of the market (2). *The Art Newspaper, 193*, 31.

Vogel, C. (2007a, November 14). At an enthusiastic Christie's sale, 'one million dollars is the new 10 grand'. *The New York Times*. http://www.nytimes.com/2007/11/14/arts/design/14auction.html. Accessed 15 November 2007.

Vogel, C. (2007b, November 15). Big prices for Bacon paintings lead sales of $315.9 million, a record total for Sotheby's. *The New York Times*. http://www.nytimes.com/2007/11/15/arts/15auction.html. Accessed 16 November 2007.

Chapter 2
Introduction

Abstract The *Introduction* develops the central argument of this work and provides insight into the research approach of a case study of making value and career building in contemporary visual art that departs from an economic geography and relational perspective on the organization and geography of the rising creative economy, and conceptualizes relations as forms of institutionalized practices and their strategic properties to take into account competition, selection, and an unequal distribution of rewards.

Keywords Creative economy · Making value · Career building · Case study · Contemporary visual art · Economic geography · Relationality · Institutions · Practices · Strategic properties · Competition · Unequal rewards

2.1 The Recent Momentum of Arts and Culture

In recent times arts and culture have gained momentum in the advanced capitalist societies, which is expressed by a growing convergence of cultural and economic spheres. The convergence has commonly been observed from opposing viewpoints either as economization of culture (Aspers 2009; Boltanski and Chiapello 2005) or culturalization of the economy (Amin and Thrift 2004; Lash and Urry 1994; Scott 1997).

Over the past decades cultural production and consumption as well as the number of intermediaries and services have multiplied manifold developing the arts disciplines of visual arts, performing arts, literature and music into full-blown cultural industries—contemporary public policy and academic language, so to speak (Garnham 2005; Hesmondhalgh 2007; McCarthy et al. 2005: 15). Moreover, arts and culture and other cultural and creative industries such as film, TV, radio, videogames, design, architecture, and advertising have been starting to feature prominently on both urban and regional development and research agendas (Gibson 2012; Lorenzen et al. 2008; Markusen and Gadwa 2010; Rantisi et al. 2006; O'Connor 2010). In addition to both quantitative growth and growing recognition

M. Fasche, *Making Value and Career Building in the Creative Economy*,
SpringerBriefs in Geography, DOI 10.1007/978-3-319-54030-6_2

as cultural and creative industries general economic trends such as the privatization of resources and management, and markets increasingly driven by speculation and financialization have manifested in arts and culture, too.

Vice-versa, not only traits of artistic practices and bohemian traditions but, and this is the central argument of this work, the key logics of how value of art is established and how art careers are built seem to have permeated into the wider creative economy, too. Elsewhere, these logics have been referred to as the metonymic relation of work and life (Graw 2008: 107), creative individualism based on open competition (Menger 1999: 566), the establishing of meaning, quality and value in relation to a professional world of producers, consumers and intermediaries (Danto 1964: 580), and complicity with precarity, and social and spatial inequality (Arnada et al. 2010).

This convergence of cultural and economic spheres has been part of broader economic, social and spatial shifts. These shifts have largely been described as the transition from mass production towards flexible specialization and post-Fordism (Amin 1994; Harvey 1989; Scott 1997), the formation of a new urban middle class favoring individualized over mass consumption (Bourdieu 1984; Raban 1974; Zukin 1989 [1982]), and the growth of interconnected networks of global flows and exchanges making territorial boundaries increasingly porous but not rendering places meaningless (Appadurai 1990; Castells 1996; Sassen 1991).

The post-industrial economy is characterized by a growing dominance of financial and business services, cultural, creative and knowledge industries, more flexible forms of production and labor, and individualized consumption (Amin 1994; Harvey 1989; Lash and Urry 1994; Scott 1997). The changes in the industrial organization are reflected by changes in the occupational structure. Just a few decades after the notion of "knowledge worker" (Drucker 1967) had been invented and accompanied by the prediction that major changes in society would be brought about by information (Bell 1974; Drucker 1967) the rise of a new occupational "creative class" has been observed (Florida 2002). This information-rich, creativity-led and technology-based occupational class refers to professionals working in both knowledge-based professions such as education, business, finance, healthcare and law, and in creativity- and innovation-based professions such as design, arts, media, science, research and engineering (Florida 2002: 69).

The creativity- and innovation-based workforce consists to a large extent of micro and small enterprises, self-employed persons, freelancers and interns (Oakley 2009). Their work culture breaks with conventional hierarchical systems of control and instead fosters low-entry, "boundary-less careers" (Hall 1996) that are characterized by a do-it-yourself ethos, peer recognition, cooperation and space for creativity and experiment (Boltanski and Chiapello 2005; Florida 2002: 12; Oakley 2009: 50). These "independents" (Leadbeater and Oakley 1999) often work from small offices, coffee shops, studios, co-working spaces and homes that are mostly located away from established commercial centers but in, or at least nearby, neighborhoods known for their artistic and creative scenes, amenities and trendy life-styles (Florida 2002; Grabher 2002; Ley 1996; Neff 2005). Although the creative people provide innovative and creative services and inputs to bigger companies they predominately create individual novel goods, services and experiences, which are tried and tested in their local environment and communicated and marketed, increasingly via social media, to a wider audience (Hutton 2000; O'Connor 2010: 66).

The rise of creative class occupations is closely associated with the formation of a new urban middle class that has a growing interest in artistic lifestyles, aesthetic distinctions and individualized consumption (Bourdieu 1984; Raban 1974; Zukin 1989 [1982]). These interests find expression in occupational choices and the idea of being a creator, aesthetic reflexivity, and the desire to curate one's life. Distinctions can be found everywhere in everyday life, for example it is cuisine not just food, fashion not just clothes, artworks not just decoration, projects not just jobs, designed spaces not just offices or homes, locations not just some place (Bourdieu 1984; Featherstone 1990). For the pursuit of 'being different' or 'being authentic', status is ascribed to certain objects, services, experiences and locations. People are not only conspicuous about their consumption and lifestyles and try to keep up with the latest trends (Veblen 1934 [1899]), this attitude increasingly also refers to production in the cultural and creative industries and craft (Ocejo 2012). Yet, the more people do this or that or like this or that the less difference or distinction there is as both the significance of individual taste or choice and its associated higher status get slowly but surely eroded (Fasche 2006: 154). Thus, there is a need for ongoing differentiation of existing and invention of new products, services, experiences and places that can be marketed, or valued, as the 'new thing' to maybe become a major trend, a new lifestyle or the next place to be for the wider urban middle class (Lash and Lurry 2007; Molotch 2002; Pratt 2008; Oakley 2009: 29).

Taken together, occupational choices for careers in the cultural, creative and knowledge industries that follow intrinsic motivations and build on success of individual creativity and talent, as well as individualized consumption, aestheticisation of everyday life, and the curation of the self, seemingly emulate traits conventionally associated with artistic practices and bohemian traditions (Boltanski and Chiapello 2005; McRobbie 2004; O'Connor 2010: 38; Zukin 1989 [1982]). In other words, arts and culture have moved right into the center of the post-industrial societies.

2.2 The Momentum of Arts and Culture in Perspective

Although there is no doubt about the growing relevance of arts and culture in the post-industrial societies regarding its praise views differ. Here, the focus is on two stylized and seemingly opposing but in fact closely interrelated perspectives, or in other words two sides of the same coin: the role of cultural and creative industries for economic growth and prosperity, and their capitalist realities of social and spatial inequality and precarity.

The first perspective follows the maxim that innovation, creativity and knowledge are the key drivers of competitiveness, growth, and prosperity in the post-industrial economy (Florida 2002; Glaeser 2011; Scott 2008). This dynamic is expressed by expanding production and consumption, growing employment numbers and increasing turnovers in the cultural and creative industries—all of which are contributing to both wealth and gross domestic products (Howkins 2001; O'Connor 2010: 37; Pratt 2008). The low entry and self-managed careers in the cultural and creative occupations are liberating by offering opportunities for everyone to follow intrinsic motivations and unique individual interests rather than those of organizations (Boltanski and Chiapello 2005; Hall 1996; McRobbie 2004; O'Connor 2010: 38).

Moreover, the growth of cultural and creative industries, individualized consumption, and the aestheticisation of everyday life have made the mutual relations between arts and culture and the urban realm increasingly visible. The everyday practices of independent cultural and creative entrepreneurs (Fasche 2006; Lange 2005; Pratt 2009), large-scale so-called flagship cultural developments (Baniotopoulou 2001; Evans 2003; Hamnett and Shoval 2003) and distinct consumption and lifestyle patterns shape and impact the urban realm. Artistic and cultural scenes, amenities and lifestyles offer information and learning resources for creativity- and innovation-based workers (Currid 2007; Grabher 2002), attract the wider middle class that wants to keep up with the latest trends (Florida 2002), and promotes urban regeneration (Fasche 2006). Culture-led urban regeneration is commonly described as physical restorations, rising real estate values, community development, and branding of neighborhoods and cities (Landry 2000; Bell and Jayne 2004; Mommas 2004). The potential of cultural and creative industries for economic development and urban regeneration has increasingly been recognized and embraced by policy makers whose cities and regions are pressured by structural unemployment, economic and social restructuring, financial austerity, and the competition between places within and across cities and regions (Kotkin 2005; Lloyd 2006; Mommas 2004).

Yet, the second perspective, or flip side of the coin, reveals the challenges of rising precarity, and social and spatial inequality that seem to accompany the rise of the creative and knowledge economy (Frank and Cooke 1995; Sholette 2005). The flexibilization of production and labor has shifted economic reward schemes from long-term and tenured employment towards short-term employment, contract work, self-employment, freelance and even unpaid work (Menger 1999; Terranova 2000). In fact, incomes among creative workers are highly unevenly distributed as the majority of creatives earn a rather low income with their creative work whereas a small minority of creative workers earns high incomes with their creative work (Lazzarato 2007; Oakley 2009: 60). Thus, these entrepreneurial self-managed careers entail significant social and economic risks for the individual (Beck 1992; Banks 2007). The risks or so-called "dark sides" of cultural and creative work (Oakley 2009: 41) are generally described as precarious working conditions such as fluctuating and contingent work and employment, irregular and low pay, and social insecurity (Banks 2007; McRobbie 2004; Neff et al. 2005; Ross 2009). These rather unstable and unpredictable careers commonly associated with arts and culture seem to have manifested in the wider creative and knowledge economy.

Moreover, the creative workforce often chooses to live and work in areas that are up-and-coming locations and by the sum of their individual yet distinct choices and everyday activities they help putting these places on the map for a wider audience (Fasche 2006). Soon, the creatives are annexed by the wider middle class, retailers and developers, and subsequently rents and property prices are rising, so goes a common trajectory of neighborhood development from the ground up. From the other end of the spectrum, top-down so to say, the creation of new cultural institutions or cultural quarters, usually with iconic architectural design, aims to offer great cultural programming while turning the place into a thriving cultural destination leading to subsequent overall economic development and prosperity—yet experience seems to show that these desired effects are not guaranteed (Pogrebin 2009; Taylor 2007; Woronkowicz et al. 2012). In fact, both from the ground-up and top-down culture- or creativity-led regeneration of urban neighborhoods ever more often appear to be no win-win situation for the share of creative people that is unable to keep up with rising rents and property prices and a shrinking amount of affordable space, and instead fosters changes in the socio-economic compositions of these neighborhoods (Davidson 2012; Fasche and Mundelius 2010).

Hence, the growth and prosperity maxim based on creativity, knowledge and innovation seems to come at growing social costs begging the questions of *how* and *why*. How is economic value for individual works made and how are careers built in the rising creative and knowledge economy? And, why are economic rewards unequally distributed among creative and knowledge workers?

2.3 Research Approach and Outline

This work focuses on revealing *how* value is made and careers are built in the creative and knowledge economy and *why* rewards among creative and knowledge workers are unequally distributed. It is argued that the organizational and geographical logics of making value in the arts seem paradigmatic of what have become wider trends in the creative and knowledge economy in post-industrial societies. According to this argument not only traits conventionally associated with artistic practices and bohemian traditions (Boltanski and Chiapello 2005; McRobbie 2004; O'Connor 2010: 38; Zukin 1989 (1982)) but also its key logics of value making and career building have permeated into the wider creative and knowledge economy. By building on evidence from a case study of contemporary visual art, referred to as paintings, drawings, photographs, sculptures, installations, media and performance art produced by artists since World War II, this work develops a heuristic conceptual framework, tentatively called value making ecology.

This heuristic conceptual framework emerges through an explorative endeavor of building "theory from cases" (Eisenhardt and Graebner 2007) and emanates from an economic geography perspective on the organization and geography of the rising creative and knowledge economy. The conceptualization starts from a relational perspective that puts forward an emphasis on cultural production as a collective process. Yet, observations prior to this research and the empirical findings indicate that making value and career building is not only a collaborative but also a highly competitive process eventually resulting in an unequal distribution of rewards. Hence, creativity and talent are necessary but not sufficient conditions for enduring value of individual works and stable long-term individual careers; instead creativity and talent need to be valued to eventually be rewarded in relation to a professional world, ultimately resulting in unequal distribution of rewards.

Thus, to account for competition, selection and the outcome of unequal rewards in the process of making value and career building, this work conceptualizes relations as forms of institutionalized practices and their strategic properties. In doing so, this work shifts the conceptual focus from a relational perspective of links and interactions embodying the positive associations with networks such as collaboration, flexibility, self-organization, de-centralization and autonomy, seemingly featuring prominently on the research agenda in the discipline of economic geography in recent years, to the very nature of relationality itself that manifests in actor-specific practices, power relations and unequal rewards (Sunley 2008). Due to a perceived scarcity in the conceptual repertoire of economic geography to explain selection, competition and the outcome of unequal rewards, the island of economic geography was left and the author travelled through the archipelago of heterodox economic studies (Peck 2012: 113) by tracing relational and institutional thinking that had been imported into economic geography at an earlier point in time back to their disciplines of origin, sociology, 'old' institutional economics, and institutional political economy. The result of these conceptual explorations are integrated into a heuristic conceptual framework, tentatively dubbed value making ecology.

This heuristic framework may contribute to an emerging debate in economic geography about immaterial qualities such as creativity, novelty and information as central parts in the determination of economic value and individual success in the rising knowledge and creative economy. The framework may be tried and tested in future research on other professional worlds of the creative and knowledge economy, such as design, film, music, architecture, fashion, literature, and journalism, and may or may not be refined, built upon, or abandoned. Moreover, it may also inspire more travel and closer collaboration across the "heterodox archipelago" (Peck 2012: 119) to better understand and conceptualize the organization and geography of value making and career building and the outcome of unequal rewards in the rising knowledge and creative economy.

Evidence from this explorative endeavor of conceptualizing the process of making value and career building in the creative and knowledge economy are revealed over the course of three main chapters, which are framed by introduction and conclusion, a prologue and an epilogue, and followed by a making of and an appendix. This *Introduction* (Chap. 2) provides the wider discourse of the rise of the creative and knowledge economy and makes a case for selecting contemporary art as adequate example to reveal the logics underlying the process of how value is created and how careers are built and to better understand why economic rewards are unequally distributed among creative and knowledge workers. The first main chapter, *Practices of Making Value-Evidence from Gallerists* (Chap. 3), focuses on the gallerists' role as intermediaries between artists and collectors, or producers and consumers, and the strategic properties informing their day-to-day activities of raising values of contemporary artworks and building artists' careers within a wider selection system of institutions and practices. The second main chapter, *A Historical-Institutional View on Making Value* (Chap. 4), provides a perspective on continuities and change within the selection system of institutions and practices of making value of contemporary visual art and building careers since the Renaissance. It reveals how the market has become the dominant institution and gallerists an authority in the process of making value and building careers. The third main chapter, *The Organization and Geography of Making Value* (Chap. 5), builds on the two preceding chapters and develops a stylized heuristic conceptualization of the selection system of institutions and practices, tentatively called value making ecology, that facilitates the competitive process of raising values of contemporary artworks and building artists' careers. The *Conclusion* (Chap. 6) summarizes the main findings of this work, speculates about potential contributions, and sketches avenues for future research emerging from this work. *Prologue* (Chap. 1) and *Epilogue* (Chap. 7) provide brief descriptions of contemporary art market history highlighting how the largely self-regulating selection system of institutions and practices of making value and career building is dominated by the market and its cycles of art market boom and bust. The *Making Of* (Chap. 8) offers insight into the explorative character of this work and the research process of building theory from cases. The *Appendix* reveals the names and venues of 18 gallerists in three cities, Los Angeles, New York City and Berlin, whose insight builds the empirical foundation of this work.

References

Amin, A. (Ed.). (1994). *Post-Fordism: A reader*. Oxford: Blackwell.

Amin, A., & Thrift, N. (2004). Introduction. In Amin, A., & Thrift, N. (Eds.), *The Blackwell cultural economy reader* (pp. i–xxx). Malden, MA: Blackwell.

Appadurai, A. (1990). Disjunction and difference in the global cultural economy. *Theory, Culture & Society, 7*(2), 295–310.

Aranda, J., Wood, B. K., & Vidokle, A. (2010). Editorial. *e-Flux Journal, 21*(12). http://www.e-flux.com/journal/editorial-18/. Accessed 10 May 2010.

Aspers, P. (2009). Knowledge and valuation in markets. *Theory and Society, 38,* 111–131.

Baniotopoulou, E. (2001). Art for whose sake? Modern museums and their role in transforming societies: The case of the Guggenheim Bilbao. *Journal of Conservation and Museum Studies, 7,* 1–15.

Banks, M. (2007). *The politics of cultural work*. Basingstoke: Palgrave Macmillan.

Beck, U. (1992). *Risk society: Towards a new modernity*. Trans. Mark Ritter. New Delhi: Sage.

Bell, D. (1974). *Coming of post-industrial society: A venture in social forecasting*. London: Heinemann.

Bell, D., Jayne, M. (Eds.). (2004). *City of quarters: Urban villages in the contemporary city*. Aldershot: Ashgate.
Boltanski, L., & Chiapello, E. (2005). *The New Spirit of Capitalism*, transl. Gregory Elliott. London and New York: Verso.
Bourdieu, P. (1984). *Distinction*. Cambridge, MA: Harvard University Press.
Castells, M. (1996). *The rise of the network society*. Oxford, Malden MA: Blackwell.
Currid, E. (2007). *The warhol economy: How fashion, art, and music drive New York city*. New York: Princeton University Press.
Danto, A. (1964). The artworld. *Journal of Philosophy, 61,* 571–584.
Davidson, A. (2012, June 5). Can mom- and pop-shops survive extreme gentrification? *The New York Times*. http://www.nytimes.com/2012/06/10/magazine/can-mom-and-pop-shops-survive-extreme-gentrification.html. Accessed June 6 2012.
Drucker, P. (1967). *The effective executive*. New York: Harper & Row.
Eisenhardt, K. M., & Graebner, M. E. (2007). Theory building from cases: Opportunities and challenges. *Academy of Management Journal, 50*(1), 25–32.
Evans, G. (2003). Hard-branding the cultural city—From Prado to Prada. *International Journal of Urban and Regional Research, 27*(2), 417–440.
Fasche, M. (2006). Creative people and gentrification: "Sowing the seeds of demise?" Evidence from Newtown, Sydney. *Erdkunde, 2,* 147–156.
Fasche, M., & Mundelius, M. (2010). *Wert der Kunst im Reuterkiez, Neukölln*. Report prepared for Neighborhood Management Reuterplatz, Berlin-Neukoelln. http://www.reuter-quartier.de/uploads/media/Wert_der_Kunst_01.pdf. Accessed 10 October 2012.
Featherstone, M. (1990). *Consumer culture and postmodernism*. London: Sage.
Florida, R. (2002). *The rise of the creative class*. New York: Basic Books.
Frank, R. H., & Cook, P. J. (1995). *The winner-take-all society*. New York: The Free Press.
Garnham, N. (2005). From cultural to creative industries. An analysis of the implications of the "creative industries" approach to arts and media policy making in the United Kingdom. *International Journal of Cultural Policy, 11*(1), 15–29.
Gibson, C. (2012). Cultural economy: Achievements, divergences, future prospects. *Geographical Research, 50*(3), 282–290.
Glaeser, E. (2011). *Triumph of the city: How our greatest invention makes us richer, smarter, greener, healthier, and happier*. The Penguin Press.
Grabher, G. (2002). Cool projects, boring institutions: Temporary collaboration in social context. *Regional Studies, 36*(3), 205–214.
Graw, I. (2008). *Der grosse Preis. Kunst zwischen Markt und Celebrity Kultur*. Freiburg: DuMont.
Hall, D. T. (1996). *The career is dead-Long live the career: A relational approach to careers*. San Francisco: Jossey-Bass Publishers.
Hamnett, C., & Shoval, N. (2003). Museums as 'flagships' of urban development. In Hoffman, L. M., Judd, D., & S. S. Fainstein (Eds.), *Cities and visitors: Regulating people, markets, and city space*. Oxford: Blackwell.
Harvey, D. (1989). *The condition of postmodernity*. Oxford: Blackwell.
Hesmondhalgh, D. (2007). *The cultural industries* (2nd ed.). London and Los Angeles: Sage.
Howkins, J. (2001). *The creative economy*. London: Penguin.
Hutton, T. (2000). Reconstructed production landscapes in the postmodern city: Applied design and creative services in the metropolitan core. *Urban Geography, 21*(4), 285–317.
Kotkin, J. (2005, October). Uncool cities. *Prospect,* 115.
Landry, C. (2000). *The creative city*. London: Earthscan.
Lange, B. (2005). Socio-spatial strategies of culturepreneurs. The example of Berlin and its new professional scenes. *Zeitschrift fuer Wirtschaftsgeographie 49*, (2), 79–96.
Lash, S., & Lurry, C. (2007). *Global culture industry*. Cambridge: Polity.
Lash, S., & Urry, J. (1994). *Economies of signs and space*. London: Sage.
Lazzarato, M. (2007). Strategies of the political entrepreneur. *SubStance, 36*(1), 87–97.
Leadbeater, C., & Oakley, K. (1999). *The independents: Britain's new cultural entrepreneurs*. London: Demos.

Ley, D. (1996). *The new middle class and the remaking of the central city*. Oxford: Oxford University Press.

Lloyd, R. (2006). *Neo-Bohemia: Arts and commerce in the post-industrial city*. New York: Routledge.

Lorenzen, M., Scott, A. J., & Vang, J. (2008). Editorial: Geography and the cultural economy. *Journal of Economic Geography, 8*(5), 589–592.

Markusen, A., & Gadwa, A. (2010). Arts and culture in urban or regional planning: A review and research agenda. *Journal of Planning Education and Research, 29*(3), 379–391.

McCarthy, K. F., Ondaatje, E. H., Brooks, A., & Szántó, A. (2005). *A portrait of the visual arts. Meeting the challenges of a new era*. Santa Monica, CA: RAND Corporation.

McRobbie, A. (2004). Creative London, Creative Berlin: Notes on making a living in the new cultural economy. http://www.ateliereuropa.com/2.3_essay.php. Accessed 13 October 2005.

Menger, P.-M. (1999). Artistic labour markets and careers. *Annual Review of Sociology, 25*, 541–574.

Molotch, H. (2002). Place in product. *International Journal of Urban and Regional Research, 26* (4), 665–688.

Mommaas, H. (2004). Cultural clusters and the post-industrial city: Towards the remapping of urban cultural policy. *Urban Studies, 41*(3), 507–532.

Neff, G. (2005). The changing place of cultural production: The location of social networks in a digital media industry. *The Annals of the American Academy of Political and Social Science, 597*(1), 134–152.

Neff, G., Wissinger, E., & Zukin, S. (2005). Entrepreneurial labor among cultural producers: "Cool" jobs in "hot" industries. *Social Semiotics, 15*(3), 307–334.

Oakley, K. (2009). *'Art works'—Cultural labour markets: A review of the literature*. London: Creativity, Culture and Education.

Ocejo, R. (2012). *The tradesmen: Interactive service, craft production, and the reinvention of working-class jobs*. Paper Presented at the 5th Experience the Creative Economy Conference, The Martin Prosperity Institute, University of Toronto, June 20 2012.

O'Connor, J. (2010). *The cultural and creative industries: A literature review* (2nd ed.). London: Creativity, Culture and Education.

Peck, J. (2012). Economic geography: Island life. *Dialogues in Human Geography, 2*(2), 113–133.

Pogrebin, R. (2009, December 12). In the arts, bigger buildings may not be better. *The New York Times*. http://www.nytimes.com/2009/12/12/arts/design/12build.html. Accessed 14 December 2009.

Pratt, A. (2008). Cultural commodity chains, cultural clusters, or cultural production chains? *Growth and Change, 39*(1), 95–103.

Pratt, A. (2009). Urban regeneration: From the arts 'feel good' factor to the cultural economy: A case study of Hoxton. *London. Urban Studies, 46*(5&6), 1041–1061.

Raban, J. (1974). *Soft city*. London: Hamish Hamilton.

Rantisi, N., Leslie, D., & Christopherson, S. (2006). Guest editorial. Placing the creative economy: scale, politics, and the material. *Environment and Planning A, 38* (10), 1789–1797.

Ross, A. (2009). *Nice work if you can get it: Life and labor in precarious times*. New York City: NYU Press.

Sassen, S. (1991). *The global city: New York, London, Tokyo*. Princeton (NJ): Princeton University Press.

Scott, A. J. (1997). The cultural economy of cities. *International Journal of Urban and Regional Research, 21*(2), 323–339.

Scott, A. J. (2008). *Social economy of the metropolis: Cognitive-cultural capitalism and the global resurgence of cities*. Oxford: Oxford University Press.

Sholette, G. (2005). Heart of darkness. A journey into the dark matter of the art world. In Hall, J. R., Stimson, B., & Becker, L. T. (Eds.), *Visual worlds* (pp. 116–138). New York and London: Routledge.

Sunley, P. (2008). Relational economic geography: A partial understanding or a new paradigm? *Economic Geography, 84*(1), 1–26.

Taylor, K. (2007. November 6). If you build it, will they come? *The New York Sun*. http://www.nysun.com/arts/if-you-build-it-will-they-come/65906/. Accessed 10 February 2012.

Terranova, T. (2000). Free labor: Producing culture for the digital economy. *Social Text, 18*(2), 33–58.

Veblen, T. (1934 [1899]). *The theory of the leisure class: An economic study in the evolution of institutions*. New York: Macmillan.

Woronkowicz, J., Joynes, C. D., Frumkin, P., Kolendo, A., Seaman, B., Gertner, R., & Bradburn, N. (2012). *Set in stone. Building America's new generation of arts facilities, 1994–2008*. Chicago: Cultural Policy Center.

Zukin, S. (1989 [1982]). *Loft living: Culture and capital in urban change*. Baltimore: Rudgers.

Chapter 3
Practices of Making Value—Evidence from Gallerists

Abstract The first out of three main chapters, *Practices of Making Value—Evidence from Gallerists*, presents results from the conceptualization of day-to-day activities of commercial gallerists. The chapter builds on empirical data derived from interviews with commercial gallerists in three cities, Berlin, New York and Los Angeles, and reveals strategic properties that inform practices of raising the value of artworks and building long stable artists' careers while mediating between aesthetic vision and sustaining their business.

Keywords Art market · Commercial gallerists · Aesthetic vision · Making value · Artists' careers · Practices · Strategic properties

Commercial galleries and auction houses are the main venues for selling and purchasing contemporary artworks. During the past decade the market was equally divided between galleries and auction houses both accounting for a 50% share of all sales of contemporary visual artworks (McAndrew 2011: 15). While auction houses focus on speculative resales artworks at galleries are usually sold for the first time. Sales at both galleries and auctions capitalize on the value of artists and their artworks embodied in the artwork's provenance and the artist's biography built by the record of exhibitions, reviews, and acquisitions for public and private collections. Yet, while competitive bidding drives prices at auctions, often resulting in record prices, gallerists raise price levels slowly and consistently with the career development of the individual artist (Velthuis 2005). Auction prices are publicly announced, while gallerists conduct sales discretely by gentleman's agreement with final prices usually remaining confidential between seller and buyer.

Gallerists, who are the focus here, aim to promote their aesthetic vision by building the careers of their artists and raising the values of their artworks, and in a reciprocal manner build their own career and gallery business. They execute a subtle dimension of power by selecting artists for their gallery programs from a wider pool of artists and thus pre-select what may subsequently be recognized, reviewed, exhibited or sold (Bystryn 1978; DiMaggio 1977: 442; White 1993), or in other words, what may become more valuable. Yet, success among galleries is

M. Fasche, *Making Value and Career Building in the Creative Economy*, SpringerBriefs in Geography, DOI 10.1007/978-3-319-54030-6_3

extremely biased. The top 2–5% of all gallerists account for half of the value of all sales by galleries (McAndrew 2011: 15), 10–15% are perceived to make substantial profits, while the rest of gallerists make very little if any profit seemingly working under similar precarious conditions like the majority of artists (Friese 2012).

For this work, 18 gallerists were interviewed with regard to their everyday practices of making value and building careers, five in Berlin, five in Los Angeles, and eight in New York. All but one gallery were located in emerging or established gallery clusters within these cities (Fig. 3.1).

Six interviewed gallerists were involved with either a second gallery or a project space in either the same city or another city; half of the interviewees had moved their gallery to another location once, one of them had already moved twice. The interviewed gallerists had been running their galleries between just one and 32 years, the average age of the galleries was nine years. All galleries were micro-businesses employing between one and six persons, one gallery had 14 employees, and supplementing this labor force by freelancers and interns on a flexible basis—being representative for the organizational structure of galleries in general (McAndrew 2011: 16). In terms of their career status the 18 interviewees could be distinguished into eight emerging gallerists, nine mid-career gallerists and maybe one, if any, superstar gallerist. The sample has two biases—but one may compensate the other. On the one hand there is a lack of superstar gallerists among the interviewees but on the other hand the sample is biased towards enduring businesses. According to general data, 66% of small businesses survive their first two years, 44% survive their first four years in business, while only 31% make it

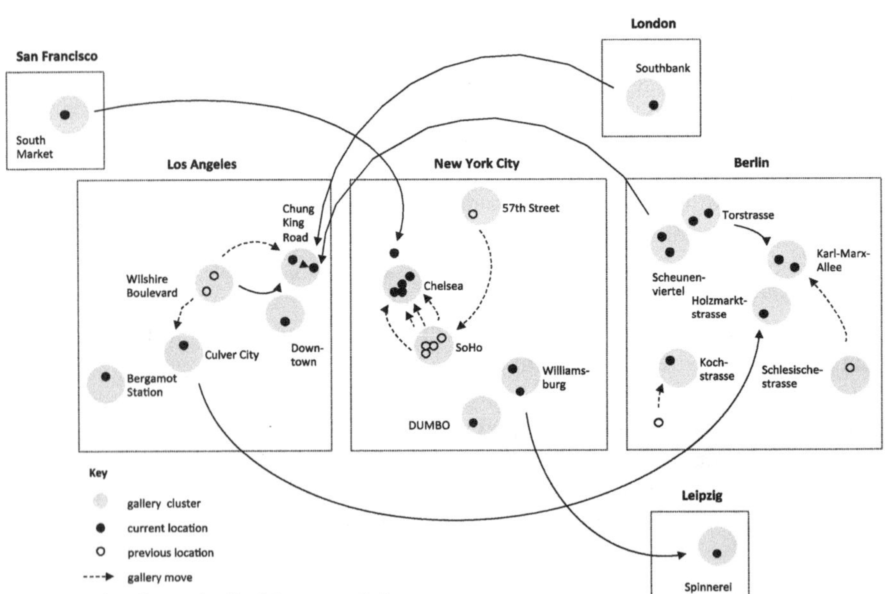

Fig. 3.1 Current and previous gallery locations of interviewed gallerists

past seven years (Knaup and Piazza 2007 quoted in McAndrew 2011: 21)—and in the sample ten gallerists or 55% of all interviewees had been running their galleries for seven years or longer.

The interviews revealed that the gallerists are driven by their passion for art. However, on a day-to-day basis they have to mediate between their aesthetic vision and sustaining their business, or between emotion and reason. The gallerists appeared intentional and strategic with regard to their everyday practices according to the best of their knowledge of institutionalized practices—or how to do things—and constantly refine their practices. According to the interview analysis the everyday practices of making value and career building are characterized by relationality as well as reciprocity, relativity, positionality, reflexivity, and contingency.

3.1 Entrepreneurial Passion and Pain

Most interviewed gallerists showed a strong entrepreneurial spirit emphasized by the notion of being "*independent*" and stressed in quotes such as "*I do my own thing*", "*I am an independent entrepreneur*" and "*not [being] joiny*" in terms of professional associations. All interviewed gallerists are driven by a passion for art rather than monetary goals as this interviewee explained,

> I am not a gallerist to accumulate fortunes; I am a gallerist, because it is a lot of fun and because I am interested in intellectual dialogue and because I want my artists to have long stable careers in contrast to somehow short super steep careers, which bring a lot of money, but short super steep careers often crash badly.

And another gallerist confirmed by sharing their observation that

> for most galleries I know, it is very important to allow space for the art and not so much about financial success.

The interviewees said that the collectors they work with are affected by art and passionate about individual artworks rather than following investment purposes even if they may have pursued investment goals in the first place expressed by the following quotes,

> all these hedge fund guys coming in and wanna buy stuff, and you know it's a trophy thing … they think they come for the money and the show, but it gets into their heads because inevitably good art does affect you,

and

> [the collectors] don't really look at art as investment that's gonna triple over the next three years, they just really fall in love with the piece and just wanna have it in their house.

All interviewed gallerists said that they seek a long-term perspective or enduring value for their artists and their artworks as well as for themselves emphasized by the notion of "*timelessness*" and quotes like,

> the ultimate goal is to integrate my artists into art history,

and

> legendary, Mohammed Ali kinda shit, you know man, we own this joint, it's all on baby.

However, the interviewees admitted the challenges of promoting their aesthetic vision as two interviewees confessed,

> that's the hard part to sort of balance trying to get sales and building the artists' careers,

and

> the experience that you sell your first artwork after six months, not everyone is surviving this economically (laughing), you have to work hard, I didn't expect that.

Other interviewees revealed, "*the factor of self-exploitation is huge*". This tension between promoting their aesthetic vision by raising the value of their artists' artworks and building their artists' careers, and sustaining their businesses, or between emotion and reason, informs their everyday practices of making value and building careers.

3.2 Everyday Practices of Making Value

There are no entry barriers to become a gallerist. No formal education is required. Degrees or certificates are not needed to open a gallery. Literally everyone could become a gallerist, one only seems to need the financial means to rent or buy a space and call it a gallery. The ways of how the interviewees became gallerists ranged from accidently stepping into it as artists or curators, emphasized by the following quote,

> I saw a sign there is a gallery space available … my studio is [outside the city] … I wanted to have a show in the city so I called to see if I could rent the space, you know on a temporary basis … they said no, they only rent to gallery owners (laughing), that was pretty subtle, right? What does it take, you know? A deposit. So basically I jumped in,

to making an intentional shift from other creative professions, or having previously worked in the art world as employee either at an alternative space or established gallery.

In other words, the knowledge of institutionalized practices of making value of artworks and building artists' careers, or knowing how to do things, varied significantly at the respective beginnings of their careers as gallerists. The knowledge ranged from those who had learned from gallerists they had previously worked with emphasized by the following quote,

> Leo Castelli, the legendary dealer, teached me how to do stuff,

to those who did not know much about how to perform the role of a gallerist emphasized by quotes such as

> I had no idea what the business is like,

and

> it is a learning process.

The analysis of everyday practices of commercial gallerists revealed six strategic properties of making value of contemporary visual art and building artists' careers (Fig. 3.2). The practices of making value are not just relational, or collaborative, as sometimes over-simplified, but equally characterized by reciprocate, positional, relative, reflexive, and contingent properties accounting for the highly competitive and long-term character of establishing enduring value and building stable long-term careers. The different practices and its strategic properties are in fact overlapping and entangled with each other but in the following distinguished for analytic purposes. Practices and strategic level vary with knowledge of how to do things and the individual career stage.

Properties of making value	**Practices of making value**	***Quotes from gallerists***
relational	cooperating	*"the notion of that you can build an artist all by yourself is a ridiculous idea, way too much ego, you need help man"*
	competing	*"we all want access to the same collectors and we all meet on art fairs, so competition is not only in a city, it is international"*
reciprocate	growing together	*"the success of my artists is the success of the gallery"*
	being selective	*"I knew, if we make the move [next door to a superstar gallery] I would propel my gallery from being a small interesting gallery to becoming a major player"*
relative	observing	*"you watch them and they watch you"*
	making visible	*"you cannot be somewhere all alone"*
positional	promising	*"[it is] like a horse race, once the others are ahead, then they fall behind, well, we'll see who will make it in the long run"*
	aiming to establish	*"in the first league you have a veritable chance to better promote your vision"*
reflexive	gradually building up	*"I want my artist to have long stable careers in contrast to somehow fast super steep careers, which bring in a lot of money, but fast super steep careers often crash badly"*
	avoiding lower status	*"I don't want to go anymore [to a satellite fair] because it is only second league"*
contingent	calculating risks	*"it's one in a million to become the next star"*
	maintaining flexibility	*"things open up, you cannot anticipate"*

Fig. 3.2 Everyday practices and properties of making value

3.2.1 Relationality—Cooperating and Competing

The gallerists both cooperate and compete with each other locally and internationally. Central for the process of making value seems that it is not only about selling artworks, described as "*a quick fix*", but about facilitating a dialogue about artworks and artists, "*the intellectual thing*" in relation to the art world, emphasized by the following quote,

> this notion of you can build an artist all by yourself is a ridiculous idea, way too much ego, you need help man, internet, art fairs, all this is nice but you know, you need shows for people .... who have actually a certain think, it's not just a quick fix, it's the whole intellectual thing you have to go thru, which you can't do on the internet, which you can't do at the art fair.

The gallerists co-locate either temporary or more permanently in order to build a critical mass to becoming visible for potential collectors but also other art world stakeholder such as curators and critics. Moreover, the gallerists coordinate openings of their gallery shows to collectively promote each other and the location, often supported by maps that show the gallery locations. But not everyone is relying on a cluster effect to generating traffic, some of the gallerists work actively on creating their own traffic and becoming a destination by trying to get reviews for gallery shows. Internationally, gallerists collaborate by co-organizing shows and sharing the representation of individual artists by dividing the global market into regions, such as Europe and North America.

Yet, at the same time the gallerists also compete with each other, as one interviewee described,

> you are strong as a group ... you generate a hype, then you differentiate and individualize.

The gallerists compete for recognition by critics, curators and collectors globally,

> we all want access to the same collectors and we all meet on art fairs, so competition is not only in a city, it is international.

They also compete for the most promising artists, as one interviewee pointed out,

> established galleries don't select from art studios, they select what younger galleries have selected before them, so it's the young galleries who are really out there and who are cutting-edge, doing the initial selection.

At least one interviewed gallerist had lost an artist to a superstar gallery. And competition increases and becomes more fierce with growing success, or rising status, as this interviewee emphasized,

> it is a small market, there are many people in this market, but the important people, these are only a few, and if you want access to them, it's becoming super small,

and

> it is hard to get in.

3.2.2 *Reciprocity—Growing Together and Being Selective*

The interviewed gallerists try to grow together with their artists and collectors, emphasized by

> the success of my artists is the success of the gallery,

and with other gallerists by co-locating or collaborating over distance. The interviewed gallerists are selective about both with whom they cooperate, where and with whom they co-locate, and whom they sell to, in order to take advantage of reciprocity.

Gallerists are able to be selective about their location, provided having the financial means to buy a property or pay the rent, to associate their program and gallery with either "*young*", "*cutting-edge*", "*established*", or "*commercial*" places. Gallerists with a second gallery or project space in the same city or another city aim to build on these geographical associations to add a different flavor to their existing gallery program. Yet, young gallerists are not yet able to be very selective or strategic in with whom they collaborate but rather engage with friends and friends of friends as one described,

> we have a lot of contacts abroad, it's because of our networks, several of my friends live in New York, they studied here or elsewhere where we met, now they live in New York, some moved from Paris to New York or they move back to Paris or they are in Tokyo at the moment, because it is interesting at the moment, and this is how our network grows,

while more established gallerists are able to be more selective as these three interviewees explained,

> I prefer to cooperate with only a few galleries and have a strong network, to work closely together,

and

> I knew, if I make the move [next door to a superstar gallery] I would propel my gallery from being a small interesting gallery to becoming a major player,

and

> meanwhile I am in the position to select the collectors … it is equally important to sell and to sell to certain people, if you sell to the right people it helps the artist and the gallery … money is not enough, they have to prove their taste, what do they buy, what are their interests, are they simply attracted by the press … do they want to make money, speculators who buy a lot for re-sale at a later point … you try to avoid that this is happening to your artists.

However, the interviewees observed that their networks had changed since they started their galleries, simply because "*not everyone is growing*", or achieving higher status. Thus, the gallerists avoid co-location with galleries of relative lower status,

> younger galleries [were] not useful for me, we were already a destination … so I was good for them but they were not necessarily good for me,

and they split with artists from their gallery stable, collectors, or collaborators "*when development stops*".

3.2.3 Relativity—Observing and Making Visible

The gallerists observe their competitors but also make themselves visible emphasized by the following quote,

> you watch them and they watch you.

Most interviewees agreed that

> you cannot be somewhere all alone.

They co-locate with other gallerists in locations known for art. Yet, a few interviewed gallerists admitted that they moved too early or too late to a specific gallery cluster and thus missed the location's momentum by not being there at the right time as one interviewee reflected,

> I stayed the full time of my lease but by the time my lease ended it had become very quiet, because everyone had started to move over … if you are not there you miss opportunities … sometimes I say it was a mistake to not have gone.

All interviewed gallerists make themselves visible to a wider audience with a website and mailing list.

In addition, the gallerists chat with selected colleagues in the local gallery cluster and when they meet on art fairs, they go to openings and visit websites, all to compare their own activities to the ones of their competitors and to keep up with everybody else' activities in order to constantly evaluate everybody's relative performance in the art world as one interviewee described,

> [you look at] which galleries are cooperating, which galleries and collectors are working together, which collectors own which artwork, which artworks have which reputation, where do they re-appear in a museum context, who else is collecting these, who is talking about them, eventually you sense what is important and what is not.

Another interviewed gallerist admitted that,

> you don't look for art's sake anymore, but it's always what's behind the name.

3.2.4 Positionality—Promising and Aiming to Establish

The interviewed gallerists are aware of the competitive race for position, status and value and the long period of time it takes to establish a leading position as one interviewee expressed,

> [it's] like a horse race, once the others are ahead, then they fall behind, well, we'll see who will make it in the long run.

The interviewed gallerists know about the opportunities associated with a relative higher position,

> in the first league you have a veritable chance to better promote your [aesthetic] vision.

However, at the same time the interviewees experience difficulties in aiming to improve their relative positions, or establishing, expressed by descriptions such a "*difficulties of pressing up*" and "*staked claims*" and the following two quotes,

> you have the bonus to be new, which eventually wanes, except you make it to the next level,

and

> becoming visible is easier than moving from this visibility up into the first league, the power of resistance is growing (laughing).

In order to continue moving up to higher status gallerists make promises about their future performance based on their current relative position. Some of the gallerists reported mimicking practices of relative positioning on scale and relative performance within the professional world to keep up in the race for status and value. For example one gallerist described how they and other local colleagues were rejected to participate in a major higher status art fair. In order to be there, be visible and observe, and get associated with the first league, they collaborated with a dozen or so other galleries and founded a new satellite art fair that ran parallel to the established art fair.

Others suspected colleagues pretending to be more successful than they actually were, and thus making flawed promises about their relative position within the art world, emphasized by the following quotes,

> you always … want to say, my business is going well, I am a hero, my artists are awesome,

and

> many colleagues … always say when you ask them about things, super business or sold out, and if this were always true they were already super-rich and retired.

Yet, as one interviewee cautioned,

> at some point the truth comes out.

3.2.5 Reflexivity—Gradually Building Up and Avoiding Lower Status

The gallery business is unpredictable as one interviewed gallerist revealed,

> working towards goals, this year I make 50, next year 100, and the year after 150,000 in sales, this is hard to do in this business.

Thus, the interviewees build their businesses gradually as one interviewed gallerist explained,

> I am slowly stepping in rather than kind of trying to strike it big right away.

Most interviewed gallerists started from a locale associated with galleries and have been focusing on building trusted relationships with artists, collectors, and other art world stakeholders. The gallerists slowly grow their professional network and geographical reach by participating in art fairs, and collaborating with another gallery or opening a second space elsewhere, ideally signaling to the rest of the art world that they are gradually building up or establishing.

Being aware of the upwardly pressured race for status and value, the reflexivity of each relative position, and a longer time period of time to establish value and build stable careers, the interviewed gallerists aim to control the pace of the rise upwards while preventing falling behind. The gallerists raise price levels only slowly and consistently according to career development reflected by reviews, exhibitions, and placement in public and private collections. Price levels not backed by provenance and biography over-value the artist and their oeuvre and risk damaging the career as two interviewees described,

> I want my artists to have long stable careers in contrast to somehow fast super steep careers, which bring in a lot of money, but fast super steep careers often crash badly,

and

> a thousand dollar piece that obviously is worth more than that but they are an emerging artist and that's the price that this piece should be at right now.

At the same time the interviewed gallerists aim to avoid a relative lower status position at all costs, either when considering moving to a different location, choosing with whom to collaborate, whom to sell to, or selecting art fairs as one said,

> I don't want to go anymore [to a satellite fair] because it is only second league.

Some of the interviewed gallerists bid at auctions when collectors aim to flip contemporary artwork to capitalize on not-yet established speculative value to prevent that an artwork and the artist name get "*burnt*" in the likely event the artwork does not find a buyer.

3.2.6 Contingency—Maintaining Flexibility and Calculating Risks

The gallerists cannot foresee whether their efforts of promoting artworks and building the careers of the artists of their gallery stable will be rewarded and thus whether they are able to keep their businesses afloat since making value and building careers are reflexive but unpredictable and furthermore resulting in a highly unequal distribution of rewards. This is emphasized by the following quotes,

> it is one in a million to become the next star,

but

> things open up, you cannot anticipate,

and

> to keep things running, you need a lot of money, to be liquid, to pre-finance.

In order to cope with these contingencies the interviewees maintain flexibility to be able to take advantage of opportunities and calculate their financial risks. The gallerists keep their overheads in terms of labor costs, rent and fair participation as low as possible. Several younger, less established gallerists supplement income from selling artworks with income from other activities such as teaching, online work, hosting events, sharing their space with other, preferably more established, gallerists. Some gallerists have a silent partner who invested capital into the gallery and receives a certain dividend from the sales. Furthermore most gallerists have an inventory with additional artworks from their artists that they can sell year-round parallel to gallery shows and art fairs.

The interviewees declined that they influence the creativity of their artists to achieve better sales to help sustain their gallery. Yet, several interviewees referred to other gallerists who seem to do so. The interviewed gallerists also pointed out that the contingencies and financial pressures influence the type of art that is shown at galleries, as one interviewee emphasized,

> some art is not shown, all art that sells not so easily, experimental stuff like installations,

and speculated about a tendency to prioritize sales over critical dialogue,

> it has consequences, you cannot spend time to send material to curators, because the same time you have to sell to pay the electricity bill.

With regard to the growth of their gallery business and an increase in overhead, the interviewed gallerists appeared to be careful in expanding their geographical reach and gallery program by testing new locations on a temporary basis, participating in art fairs, showing new artists in group shows, often during the summer, and generally observing the activities in the world for a longer period of time before making any commitments.

Overall, despite the challenge of mediating between the ideal of art for art's sake, embodied in practices of promoting their aesthetic vision, raising the value of artworks and building long stable careers for their artists, and reason, manifested by the necessity of keepin their gallery business financially viable, the interviewees showed a rather pragmatic attitude towards the process of making value and building careers. One interviewee described this general sentiment with the following words:

> It's a mythos that artworks and everything in the art world is so liberal, cutting edge and critical and all that, if you look at the facts, how for example art careers grow ... it is dangerous if you think (a) that this process is fair, (b) that what you see in a museum is necessarily good art, although it is difficult to define quality, and (c) that this is happening outside a capitalist system, it is not, it is intriguedly interwoven with capitalist interests.

References

Bystryn, M. (1978). Art galleries as gatekeepers: The case of abstract expressionists. *Social Research, 45*(2), 390–408.

DiMaggio, P. (1977). Market structure, the creative process, and popular culture: Towards an organizational reinterpretation of mass culture theory. *Journal of Popular Culture, 11*(2), 436–452.

Friese, G. (2012, December 27). Schluss mit dem Anlagewahn. *Die Zeit,* 1. http://www.zeit.de/2013/01/Kunstmarktjahr-2012. Accessed 5 January 2013.

McAndrew, C. (2011). *The role of art and antique dealers: An added value.* London: Publications UK.

Velthuis, O. (2005). *Talking prices. Symbolic meanings of prices on the market of contemporary visual art.* Princeton: Princeton University Press.

White, H. C. (1993). *Careers and creativity.* Oxford: Westview Press.

Chapter 4
A Historical-Institutional View on Making Value

Abstract The second out of three main chapters, *A Historical-Institutional View on Making Value*, presents results from the conceptualization of a selection system of institutions and practices of making value and building careers. The chapter builds on the previous chapter, secondary sources, and literature and follows the key components of the selection system back in time to reveal general continuities and changes in the organization and geography of making value and building careers over the course of the past centuries. The chapter identifies Western ideals of art as key driver of making value and building careers, shows how the market with open competition and unequal rewards for individual creativity and commercial gallerists as authority has become the dominant institution in the selection system, and reflects on recent organizational and geographical shifts within the selection system.

Keywords Selection system · Institutions · Practices · Making value · Artists' careers · Competition · Creativity · Unequal rewards · Art market · Commercial gallerists · Authority · Geography

The story of art (Gombrich 2006 [1950]) is a historical continuum. Central to the history of art and value have been taste, distinctions and status, and the succession of hitherto two different frameworks of art, a utilitarian and a modern framework of art (Shiner 2001). Throughout history the definition of taste has been a competitive process for status, position and power mediated by respective selection systems of institutions and practices at respective periods of time (Baxandall 1972).

Here, a historical-institutional perspective offers insight into how the strategic properties of making value and career building and the authoritative role of the gallerist evolved by following conceptual components of a selection system of institutions and practices back in time. The conceptual components of the selection system are described as three institutions—discourse, museum, and market—unit of value, authority, reward scheme, and geography. An ex post perspective reveals general changes as well as continuities within the organization and geography of making value and building careers and puts, first, the tension between emotion and reason as key driver of the process of making value and building careers, second, the

M. Fasche, *Making Value and Career Building in the Creative Economy*, SpringerBriefs in Geography, DOI 10.1007/978-3-319-54030-6_4

market as today's dominant institution with gallerists as authority, and, third, recent organizational and geographical shifts, into a wider temporal perspective.

The historical-institutional perspective builds on the conceptualization of institutions and agency (Hodgson 2002, 2006), adds notions from historical sociology and political sciences (Martin 2010; Schneiberg 2007), and refers to recent discussions in economic geography (Grabher 2009; Hodgson 2009; Martin 2010; Sunley 2008). Central to these discussions are reflections of how to conceptualize institutional continuity and change beyond the canonical model of accidental origin and equilibrium (Hodgson 2002; Martin 2010; Schneiberg 2007) and randomness or inevitability (Hodgson 2009), as well as relational conceptualizations, or a relational capitalism, that may dismiss the stability of institutions informing practices and relations while overemphasizing the invention of new practices and overly positive connotations of connectivity itself (Sunley 2008).

Here, the ontology of a historical-institutional perspective on making value builds on assumptions of composite entity (Martin 2010), downward causation and caused agency (Hodgson 2002) expressed by continuity and incremental change through layering, conversion, and recombination within the respective framework and its selection system of institutions and practices (Martin 2010; Schneiberg 2007).

There is heterogeneity both among stakeholders and within institutions because stakeholders and institutions are in fact *composite entities* (Martin 2010: 14). Stakeholders can be very similar in key aspects but with each individual stakeholder there is "some degree of variation" either due to context or genesis (Hodgson 2009: 169). Likewise institutions consist of many different organizational elements, norms, and practices (Hodgson 2002; Schneiberg 2007). Despite these heterogeneities institutions exhibit a significant degree of order and relative stability which is enhanced by *downward causation* of institutional constraints that lead to the creation of shared beliefs and similar behaviors among stakeholders (Hodgson 2002: 111). In turn, stakeholder practices informed by shared beliefs and similar behaviors strengthen and reinforce institutions. However, in contrast to institutions stakeholders are deliberate and purposeful (Hodgson 2002) and this *caused agency* not only reinforces but also refines institutions (Hodgson 2009: 171). In fact, stakeholders may apply but also vary or even abandon institutionalized practices in order to fit with individual intentions or in reaction to general economic and social developments (Becker 2008 [1982]; Hodgson 2009; Schneiberg 2007).

From this variety of practices new habits and rules may evolve through layering, conversion and recombination to complement, adjust, tweak or even replace habits and rules in the established institutional repertoire (Hodgson 2006; Martin 2010; Schneiberg 2007). Through *layering* existing rules and habits are gradually changed by adding new rules and procedures to what already exists (Martin 2010: 14). *Conversion* and *recombination* refer to a reorientation in an institution in terms of function by either adding new layers or serving a new purpose (Martin 2010: 15; Schneiberg 2007). Layering, conversion and recombination coexist and interact. It is possible for any single institutional component to change without requiring the rest to change, but each layer, each conversion, and each recombination is a small change and a sum of small changes may—or may not—cumulate and lead to fundamental change in the selection system of institutions and practices (Martin 2010; Schneiberg 2007).

Thus, although institutions and agency are mutually entwined, institutions themselves are in fact outcomes of previously institutionalized practices, interactions and intentions, yet without being consciously designed (Hodgson 2002). In other words, each institutional novelty builds on a preceding institution rather than accidently appearing out of nowhere; in fact, there is infinite regress within an open-ended framework with ongoing processes of continuity and change (Hodgson 2006). Hence, continuity and change are neither random nor inevitable but path-dependent (Hodgson 2009). Thus, the institutions and practices of making value reveal a significant degree of continuity and relative stability while co-evolving incrementally rather than inhering in equilibrium (Hodgson 2006; McCarthy et al. 2005; Shiner 2001; White and White 1993 [1965]).

Here, time is interrupted and divided into meaningful periods to highlight general changes and shifts as well as continuities and stabilities in the organization and geography of making value over past centuries (Fig. 4.1), first, the system change from a utilitarian framework of art to a modern framework of art that has maintained its staying power until today; second, the institutional change within the modern framework of art with the rise of the market as dominant institution and gallerists as authority, enabling creative individualism and open competition resulting in highly unequally distributed rewards; and third, the most recent shifts such as the growing influence of private collectors, and a geographical expansion to places previously not connected to the Western art world.

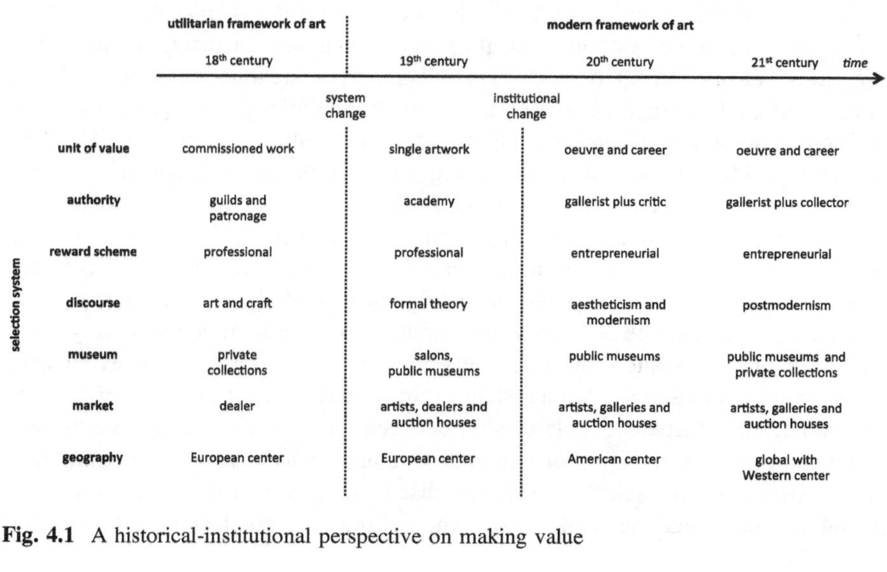

Fig. 4.1 A historical-institutional perspective on making value

4.1 The System Change—From a Utilitarian to a Modern Framework of Art

Art as we know it today is actually a more recent invention (Graw 2008; Greffe 2007; Shiner 2001). Today, art is usually associated with the prestigious category of fine art and higher status (Shiner 2001). In fact, art, as we know it today, is one of the great concepts of modern Western culture (Roelstraete 2010). Central to the Western concept of art are the ideals of fine art, artist and aesthetics. Some aspects of these ideals can already be found among ancient Greek and Roman philosophers and Renaissance painters (Shiner 2001). Yet, it was only during the course of the long 18th century in the European increasingly bourgeois and capitalist societies that these ideals coalesced into a regulative framework with respective institutions and practices that replaced the former utilitarian framework of art that had lasted for more than two thousand years (Shiner 2001). This modern framework of art became regulative only in a gradual manner of layering, conversion and recombination of rules and habits driven by an uneven and contested conjunction and concurrence of cultural, social, political and economic processes since the early Renaissance (Greffe 2007; Shiner 2001).

At the core of the transformation from the utilitarian framework of art in which any human activity performed with skill and grace had been regarded as art to the modern framework of art was the release of art from any utilitarian purpose expressed by its distinction from crafts and popular arts in terms of genres, professional status and consumption (Graw 2008; Greffe 2007; Shiner 2001). In fact, when art was released from any utilitarian purpose and idealized, it actually set the stage for projections and marketing and art came to inhere in a paradox: art connected to the economy it claims to be distinct from in the first place (Graw 2008). Hence, art is based on contradiction. It appears as "an animal struggling to find its categories" (Amin 2009) or sociological centaur, a creature composed of part human and part horse (Illouz 2005). In Greek mythology this half-human and half-animal body is described as being caught up between its two natures. The head is greedy, brutal, ruthless and calculating whereas the body longs for relation, intimacy, authenticity and self-realization. Both natures can neither be separated nor reconciled; instead there is an ongoing tension and negotiation between the two. In other words, art freed from utilitarian purpose has been colonized by economic motives ever since despite peoples' persisting efforts to realize a romantic utopia of art for art's sake. But although economic matters invade art, art is not entirely taken over by economic matters because every notion of something as art evokes the ideals of art and ascribes higher status (Graw 2008). This paradox of art, the interconnected yet irreconcilable tension between emotion and reason, can be seen as the source of the dynamic of making value and materializes in the institutions and practices of the selection system, discourse and dialogue, museums and exhibiting and collecting, and market and selling and purchasing (Illouz 2005; Shiner 2001).

The elevation of visual arts such as painting and sculpture into the category of fine arts was caused by altering practices of organizing and rewarding artistic work that led to a gradual shift of the *unit of value* from commissions or contract work to single artworks. Commissioned works had often involved many hands, usually the ones of a master and his students, and signatures on the finished piece were not yet common whereas a "work of art" was created and signed by the individual artist (Greffe 2007; Galenson 2007). Commissions were rewarded by fixed rates per day but this practice was increasingly challenged by claims to not only being paid by the amount of manual working time but also for an immaterial component of the work such as the level of invention and imagination (Galenson 2007). With this new emphasis on immaterial components the determination of rewards shifted from measurable hence objective means such as hours worked to increasingly subjective negotiable means such as authenticity, novelty and reputation—or from absolute to relative performance and from equal to more unequal economic rewards.

Yet, the status shift from manual workers working according to rule and skill to intellectual workers being inspired and having a genius was accompanied by a practice of being discrete about monetary rewards (Galenson 2007; Shiner 2001). Concerns with prices and greediness were perceived as evil to the artists' moral and the quality of work (Galenson 2007: 4) whereas in reality the new status had opened opportunities to negotiate star fees with wealthy patrons and accumulate substantial fortunes unheard before (Galenson 2007; Shiner 2001). Thus, while artists were perceived to work for the honor of patrons and academies or for the love of art itself a market in which artworks were traded by artists, middlemen and auction houses beyond the regulation of guilds, patronage and academies grew gradually but consistently (Galenson 2007; Shiner 2001).

However, while market activities were expanding the academies gained influence and eventually replaced guilds and patronage as *authority* in the definition of taste, the regulation of artistic practices and the distribution of rewards (Shiner 2001). Previously, guild associations supported careers in a professional *reward scheme* by controlling the education of master-craftsman and the organization and practices of craft making (Robertson 2005), while the tastes of wealthy patrons defined content, forms, material, colors, purpose and place of appreciation of the commissioned work (Galenson 2007). Eventually the academies dominated the institutions of discourse and museum while rejecting commercial activities, or in other words the *market,* as something of lower status (Shiner 2001). In fact, with the rise of the academies the ideals of art were institutionalized and elevated to their highest value (Shiner 2001) emphasized by aesthetically appealing artworks standing for themselves and perceived to be priceless.

However, although art was released from its utilitarian purpose artistic practices and rewards were still regulated. The academies shaped the *discourse* by defining and reinforcing a formal theory of art with a hierarchy of subject matter and correct style. In doing so, their aesthetic judgment executed power over admissions, awards, reviews, state commissions and tenured employment in a professional reward scheme (White and White 1993 [1965]). Art appreciation gradually shifted from private pleasure of wealthy patrons in private spaces to an increasingly public enjoyment for the rising bourgeois audience at exhibitions in academies and newly founded public *museums*. The Salon de Paris, an annual or biannual exhibition directed by the most prestigious academy, the École des Beaux Arts, became the central venue for an introduction to a wider audience as well as for reviews, awards, reputation build-up and legitimation and thus the integration into a canon of great works, or in other words, for positioning and comparing artworks not only in relation to formal art theory but increasingly also relative to each other and in relation to the audience (White and White 1993 [1965]).

However, the transformation from a broader utilitarian framework of art to the modern framework of art varied significantly per art genre as well as in timing and *geography*. After the 18th century the modern framework of art and its selection system of institutions and practices were largely taken for granted and subsequently spread all over Europe and America. The ideals of art—autonomy, artist-genius and aesthetics—were soon believed to be universal and both Europeans and Americans have been successful to make them so ever since (Shiner 2001).

4.2 The Institutional Change—The Rise of the Market as Dominant Institution

The market as dominant institution in the modern framework of art and selection system of institutions and practices of making value evolved in the French Painting world at the end of the 19th century. The market could rise because the academies were unable to adapt to changing social and economic conditions (White and White 1993 [1965]). Rising numbers of artists, dealers and critics and their independent activities beyond the academies and growing demand from the nouveau riche ascending with the accumulation of wealth during the Industrial Revolution gradually weakened the authority of the academies (White and White 1993 [1965]). The shift in authority from the academies to the market made possible creative individualism based on open competition that is resulting in an unequal distribution of economic rewards (Menger 1999: 566) and led to a perception that prices reflected value and career development (Plattner 1998).

With open competition the *unit of value* shifted from single artworks to the œuvre and career (White and White 1993 [1965]). The value of a single artwork became reflexive to the value of the entire body of work, the oeuvre, and found expression in reputation build-up and career development through reviews, exhibitions and sales. Ever since artists and their artworks, or person and work, have been metonymic, one standing for the other (Graw 2008: 170). Artists were no longer rewarded with tenured employment in a professional reward scheme but rewarded in an entrepreneurial *reward scheme*.

The *authority* in the modern framework of art shifted from the academies with their central institution of the École des Beaux Arts towards dealers and critics (White and White 1993 [1965]). The commercial gallerist became the central intermediary between artists and collectors by exhibiting artworks, getting reviews, and facilitating sales to build art careers and raise values and price levels of artworks (White 1993). In doing so, the gallerists emulated the patronage role of guilds while the practices of art dealing were inherited from the international trade with paintings and luxury goods via middleman in earlier centuries (White and White 1993 [1965]). Art criticism as professional activity emerged with the rise of public exhibitions and growing interest in art in the 19th century, and with the decay of the academies the role of formulating and enforcing formal art theory was passed on from artists themselves to professional critics (White and White 1993 [1965]).

The dominant venue for appreciation and legitimation shifted from academies and salons to public *museums* that were newly founded by social elites and governments. With a rising middle class, expanding interest in arts and culture, rising education levels and more leisure time, especially since World War II, the number of non-profit institutions such as public museums but also alternative spaces, Kunsthallen, arts collectives and community galleries multiplied. The public museum developed into an important civic institution of the city (McCarthy et al. 2005). In exchange to tax-exempt status or direct government funding public museums and other non-profit institutions are expected to serve the arts but also provide benefits to the community. The arts-orientated mission includes preserving, collecting, exhibiting, studying and interpreting whereas the community-orientated mission refers to education and community involvement (International Council of Museums 2006). Hence, especially public museums have been facing a tension between these two missions ever since—described as an endemic debate about the museum "being about something" versus "being for somebody" (Weil 1999: 229).

With the demise of the authority of the academies the *discourse* shifted from academism to aestheticism. Modern aestheticians claim that art is autonomous and that the judgment of taste is based on a general theory of perception. Rather than emphasizing the importance of subject matter and correct style aestheticism focuses on the beauty, universality and autonomy of artworks by distinguishing those 'works of art' worth the title from those not (Becker 2008 [1982]: 137). However, as the *market* expanded, sales and rising price levels seemed to imply cultural legitimacy (Plattner 1996: 30). The Bearskin auction in 1914 is regarded as watershed moment in the history of the art market. The Bearskin group was a group of young elite French men who had bought Impressionists collectively between 1904 and 1914. In 1914 they auctioned off these artworks for several times of the price they had originally paid. These profits from reselling or flipping artworks led to the perception that value is reflected by price. Critics had to revise and adapt the discourse to new works that initially meant to challenge the modern framework of art but were successful on the market (Becker 2008 [1982]: 137). Gradually the dominant discourse shifted from aestheticism to modernism expressed by a succession of art movements and different styles such as abstract expressionisms, pop art and minimalism (McCarthy et al. 2005).

With the creation of conceptual artworks by Marcel Duchamp, Andy Warhol and others aestheticism failed to provide rationales or explanations for the success and value of contemporary visual art altogether (Becker 2008 [1982]: 162). In order to offer an alternative answer to philosophical questions of aesthetic quality an institutional theory of art, though philosophically based but seemingly sociological, argued that the aesthetic character and the quality of art can be found outside the physical artwork in relation to an existing art world (Danto 1964; Dickie 1969). In other words, aesthetic quality manifested in an ongoing dialogue about artworks facilitated by the interrelated institutions and their practices of the three institutions: discourse and criticism, curating, scholarship; museum and collecting; and market and selling and purchasing over time and space. Thus, with creative individualism and open competition the determination of aesthetic quality shifted from a universal conception of art with value inherent in the art object to a more relational view of art-ness and value as continuous variables (Becker 2008 [1982]: 153) in a process of making value.

The judgment of aesthetic quality, or making value, became more de-central both socially by involving more and more different stakeholders and *geographically* by expanding to more and more venues and locations. After World War II and with the emigration of artists from Europe to the U.S. the art world center shifted from Paris to New York. Ever since art world events such as exhibitions, reviews and sales facilitated by the interrelated practices of different art world stakeholders in their respective venues in respective locations position artists and their artworks relative to each other to build up reputation and confer status or make value. Rising price levels for artworks are perceived as rising value and a promising art career stimulating demand while falling prices are interpreted as signal for a declining art career and lowering demand (Plattner 1998). The will to pay substantial sums for artworks and more and more artists entering the competition give rise to an upwardly pressured race for status and value, or more central positions, resulting in a highly uneven distribution of rewards.

Moreover, the success of the Impressionists whose works were heavily criticized at first but selling at high prices at a later time seemed to prove that going against the dominant discourse, or challenging the modern framework of art and its institution and practices could eventually be profitable. This perception became embodied in the story of the rejected artist whose work is ultimately recognized for its greatness and rewarded accordingly (Plattner 1998). This story has been passed on and finds expression in a success of art movements during the 20th century and artists continuing to make art rather than being devastated by negative criticism or absent market success but pursuing the ideal that creativity can only flourish when autonomous, or far away from the market.

4.3 Recent Developments—Organizational and Geographical Shifts

The past decades have been characterized by quantitative growth and geographical expansion of the art world and an increasing dominance of the market within the selection system of institutions and practices of making value. The number of artists, collectors and those mediating between supply and demand as well as the number of venues and events where artworks are shown to the public increased far and wide and expanded the art world well beyond its Western center (McCarthy et al. 2005: xvii). In addition, a specialized art service industry of art advisors, shipping companies, insurance experts, storage services, and public relation companies has evolved to support the activities of the art world (McCarthy et al. 2005). In other words, contemporary visual art has developed into a creative industry.

Moreover, ever since the rise of the modern art market volumes of sales and price levels have been soaring, driven by growing demand, liquidity and speculation on future value and embedded in cycles of market boom and bust. The growing dominance of the market is reflected by shifting roles and new practices within the institutions of the selection system such as the rising influence of private collectors in showing and legitimating contemporary visual art (Fasche 2013), auction houses rivaling galleries in selling contemporary visual art (McCarthy et al. 2005), and growing global competition for status and value due to ever more stakeholders and venues in ever more locations entering the competition, many of them working independently and rewarded in an entrepreneurial reward scheme (Frank and Cook 1995).

The success of the Scull auction in 1973 (Fig. 4.2) is perceived as another watershed moment in the history of the *market* of contemporary visual art spurring financialization—growing liquidity, rising price levels and speculation on future value—of the process of making value of contemporary visual art (Plattner 1996: 35). The high sum the Sculls earned with this auction and subsequent market success of the artists whose works were auctioned nurtured a perception that prices not only reflect value but that value could be raised by prices and money made from flipping contemporary artworks at auction. In other words, rising price levels for artists and their artworks were no longer perceived just as a signal of a promising art career but believed to increase the value of the artist's oeuvre and develop artists' careers. Previously artists in the U.S. had little prospect of making money with their artworks, but in the wake of the Scull auction art careers seemed not only be possible but also well rewarded.

In the 1980s auction houses changed their practices by beginning to resell contemporary visual art and thus started to rival galleries as venue for distributing contemporary artworks (McCarthy et al. 2005). In contrast to gallerists who raise price levels according to reputation build-up with reviews, exhibitions and acquisitions, sales at auctions are driven by speculative bidding. With price levels for living artists at auctions rising and increasingly subject to speculation on future value the pressure on gallerists is growing since the price level for artworks is not allowed

In 1973 the New York taxi tycoon Robert C. Scull and his wife Ethel consigned a big part of their Pop art collection, 50 paintings and sculptures, to Sotheby's New York. The couple were among the first collectors buying Pop art way before New York's cultural tastemakers realized that Pop art was the next big thing (Kaplan 2010). The Sculls earned a total of US $2.2 million with this auction, surpassing many times the prices they had once paid for these artworks at galleries and in art studios. The auction prices may appear rather low by today's standards but back then many prices were auction records for the living artist at auction. Jasper John's "Double White Map" once bought for US $10.000 sold for US $240.000, an auction record for a living artist at the time, Robert Rauschenberg's "Thaw" once bought for US $900 sold for US $85.000 and Andy Warhol's "Flowers" once purchased for US $3.500 sold for US $135.000 (Panero 2009).

The reactions to the auction and its prices were mostly raging. The New York Magazine railed that the "banal nouveau riche" whose "greed", "shamelessness" and "sheer, unadulterated chutzpah" killed contemporary visual art this auction (Kaplan 2010). Word of mouth passed on that the artist Robert Rauschenberg arrived drunken and furious at the auction house and shouted at Robert Scull "it was only love, this is the divorce, I've been working my ass off just for you to make that profit", but Scull replied "it works for you too, Bob, now I hope you'll get even bigger prices" (Panero 2009).

History seemed to have proved Robert Scull to be true: although the artists didn't benefit directly from this particular auction, rising price levels for artworks by Robert Rauschenberg, Jasper Johns, Andy Warhol and others made these artists rich men in the years following. In 2010 the Acquavella Galleries in New York put on a museum style show with 44 of the most striking artworks of the former Scull collection lent from public museums and private collectors. The press release describes the exhibition as "comprehensive portrait of the scope and quality of their taste" and thus rehabilitates the couple's reputation by referring to Robert Scull as one of the greatest collectors of American art of the post-war era (Acquavella Galleries 2010). And auction success has continued: Andy Warhol's silkscreen "200 One Dollar Bills" which sold for US $385.000 at the estate auction after Robert Scull's death in 1986 fetched US $46 million at Sotheby's New York in 2009 (Melikian 2009).

Fig. 4.2 Financialization—The Scull auction at Sotheby's New York in 1973

to go down as this may signal the decline of an art career. Thus, during boom times it is difficult to prevent over-speculation on future value and excesses of price levels while during recession it is challenging to prevent deflation and maintaining price levels. Nonetheless, the gallerists are still dominant and perform the role of authority in the process of making value, they scout and select new talent for their gallery programs, they build art careers and raise values by getting reviews and exhibitions, and placing artworks in public and private collections (McCarthy et al. 2005).

Yet, in 2008, the artist Damien Hirst challenged the art market rules by cutting out his gallerists and partnered with an auction house to auction hundreds of new artworks from his art studio (Fig. 4.3). Auction houses usually only facilitate the resale of contemporary artworks that is at least five years old. Hirst's gallerists ended up supporting the auction sale for the sake of the relationships with their collectors and with the artist himself and the income his artworks provide for the galleries. There were rumors that the Japanese artist Takashi Murakami may

In September 2008 an auction sale at Sotheby's London not only ended with a record sale by a single artist at auction but also stretched the art market rules, causing unease among art world stakeholders whether other artists may follow suit and provoking a debate about the commodification of contemporary visual art.

The Damien Hirst auction sale "Beautiful Inside My head Forever" of 200+ new artworks straight from the art studio broke with the unwritten rules of 'Do not doge your dealer' and 'Do not auction anything that has not been sold or bought before or is less than five years old' (Economist 2008: 87). Gallerists had been supporting Hirst's career for nearly 20 years. They introduced him to wider and wider audiences and build his reputation and the one of his artworks by placing his artworks in prestigious public and private collections. However, for this particular sale Hirst decided to bypass his gallerists and the obligations these partnerships imply and instead used the auction house as alternative channel of distribution in order to reach new collectors and maximize his profits (Bevan 2008).

The auction sale was a high risk event as the sale was not guaranteed by the auction house or another party (Vogel 2008). No one knew whether there would be enough demand for such a quantity of artworks and whether the price levels that 'Hirsts' had to come to command would be reached. According to rumours his London gallery was already sitting on 200 unsold artworks (Economist 2008:89). Moreover, back then Hirst's œuvre still lacked the validation of a major retrospective in a prestigious public museum (Thornton 2008). A failing auction sale could have been a fatal signal for his career and the price level of his artworks. But the auction sale surpassed expectations. All but five of 223 lots sold earning an exorbitant total of $200 million.

Fig. 4.3 Off-path experimentation—The Hirst auction sale at Sotheby's London in 2008

facilitate a similar auction sale, but no artist followed suit yet, except that, in fact, less visible from a Western centric perspective, artists in India and China are regularly selling their artworks via auction houses rather than galleries. Although Hirst's off-path experiment may not change the market rules any time soon, his experimental activity has been recognized by the other two institutions, discourse and museum. One year after the auctions sale, a major travelling Pop Art show "Pop Life" organized and curated by Tate London in cooperation with Kunsthalle Hamburg included Hirst's auction sale into the exhibition and related his off-path experiment to Andy Warhol's ideas of business and art.

However, high prices for contemporary artworks at auction can be increasingly mistaken for enduring value and an established career. Artists can become successful more quickly through auction sales but high prices are no guarantee for enduring value of artworks and a long stable career since neither the artist nor the artwork have passed the test of time still central in stabilizing prices (McCarthy et al. 2005). In other words, price as signal of status and value is increasingly inflated. Naturally, the sum of overall status cannot be improved (Frank 1985)—but price levels can. In this sense ever more rising price levels are primarily an expression of growing competition and aiming to keep up with the Joneses in the race for status and value among private collectors (Frank and Cook 1995). Thus, the entrepreneurial, the winner-take-all *reward scheme* seems to have evolved from a stylized pyramid into more of a high-spike-long-tail-end model with a very high spike of seemingly ever-rising price levels at galleries and auctions, and a long tail end lower part with self- marketing activities of artists.

The *discourse* has shifted from modernism to post-modernism, the absence of any dominant single theory, genre, form, or aesthetic of pre-determined higher status. The pluralization of the discourse gave way to the coexistence and competition of an unprecedented range of artistic practices such as painting, sculpture, photography, installation, performing art, and media art (Plattner 1998). Literally everything can be valued as art. The proliferation of what can be art has led pessimistic voices to speculate about a death of "real" art. Others, in turn, celebrate post-modernism as liberation from the normative ideals of the modern framework of art. Ever new forms of art and movements of resistance tried to undermine the ideals of the modern framework of art, but despite their critical stance their activities emulate the practices of the very same selection system of institutions and practices. Moreover, the works of those challenging the ideals of fine art got quickly been absorbed into the "Church of Art" and the very canons they initially meant to resist (Shiner 2001: 8). In fact, the art market seems to actively discover and support alternative, subversive and independent forms of artistic production (Hesmondhalgh 2007).

More recently public *museums* have started to loose power in the process of making value (Fasche 2013, Pes 2011). Public museums are increasingly challenged by financial pressure stemming foremost from higher acquisitions costs with rising price levels for artworks on the market and growing operation costs because of a recent museum extension designed by a star architect, declining revenues and support from governments and donors, and increasing competition for visitors, donations and bequests due to a global museum boom (McCarthy et al. 2005). To cope with these pressures public museums increasingly cooperate with gallerists and private collectors by loaning artworks from galleries and private collections for public museum exhibitions. This practice is contested among art world stakeholders because gallerists and private collectors are suspected to take advantage of public museums shows that may raise the value for artists and artworks and translate into higher prices at galleries and auctions (Lind 2010).

Wealthy private collectors have a growing influence in what is shown to the public and gain power, or *authority*, in the process of making value of artists and their artworks by having more purchasing power and abandoning the conventional practices of donating artworks and entrusting collections to a public museum and instead perform the legitimating and historicizing role of public museums themselves (Kallir 2007; Pollock and Adam 2008). Wealthy private collectors have started to pursue more comprehensive philanthropic missions by building their own museums, often iconic buildings designed by a star architect, and emulating the scholarly and social role of public museums. Private museums usually show the collector's collection to the public, employ curators, publish catalogues, offer educational programmes and engage with the local community. These activities are central in places without a tradition of public museums and where public access to contemporary visual art is limited (Adam 2011).

The growing influence of wealthy private collectors in making value and career building causes unease that money may trump art historical scholarship. The worst fears are those of an art historical canon shaped by a few superstar collectors lacking sophisticated taste and substantial art historical knowledge and rather interested in signature architectural designs than solid museum programming. These fears reflect enduring Western ideals of art being autonomous and public museums being pristine institutions (Adam 2011). In fact, wealthy private collectors have been influential on the art historical canon ever since the Renaissance (Lind 2010). The founding stones of public museums in the early 20th century were often private, feudal or Church collections of commissioned work and artwork purchases. Today's public museum collections could not have been built with donations and bequests and access to supporting audiences in central art world locations such as New York City, London and Paris from early on (Quemin 2006). Over the course of the 20th century a few of these public museums developed into public superstar museums now preserving the most prestigious art collections worldwide and enjoying the historic advantage of the reputation, or status, of their world famous collections over younger public and private museums. To date, an integration into the collection of a public superstar museum such as The Museum of Modern Art (MoMA), the Salomon R. Guggenheim Museum in New York, Tate Modern in London, or Centre Pompidou in Paris has still more legitimation power than integration into a private collection.

Thus, in fact, until today the modern framework of art and its selection system of institutions and practices has maintained its most general characteristics and staying power even though its institutions and practices and geography of making value and building careers have been evolving and heavily contested over the course of the last two centuries (Shiner 2001). In a globally expanding art world it remains to be seen whether Western ideals of art and its institutions and practices of making value and building careers will be adopted, recombined, blurred, or even abandoned in places previously not connected to the Western art world.

References

Acquavella Galleries. (2010). *Robert & Ethel Scull: Portrait of a Collection*. Press Release.

Adam, G. (2011, June 8). Art market analysis: Are domestic collectors ready to take the world? *The Art Newspaper, 225*.

Amin, A. (2009). *Culture and the urban economy: Spectacle, driver, entanglement?* Paper presented at HafenCity University Hamburg, October 21, 2009.

Baxandall, M. (1972). *Painting and experience in fifteenth century Italy*. Oxford: Clarendon Press.

Becker, H. S. (2008 [1982]). *Art worlds*. Updated and expanded 25th Anniversary Edition. Los Angeles: University of California Press.

Bevan, R. (2008, July–August). Damien Hirst is rewriting the rules of the market (1). *The Art Newspaper, 193*, 31.

Danto, A. (1964). The artworld. *Journal of Philosophy, 61*(19), 571–584.

Dickie, G. (1969). Defining art. *American Philosophical Quarterly, 6*(3), 253–256.

Economist (2008, September 13). *Damien Hirst. The shark's last move* (pp. 87–89).
Fasche, M. (2013). Making art history—Wealthy private collectors and contemporary visual art. In Hay I. (Ed.), *Geographies of the super-rich* (pp. 171–185). London: Edward Elgar.
Frank, R. H. (1985). *Choosing the right pond: Human behavior and the quest for status*. New York: Oxford University Press.
Frank, R. H., & Cook, P. J. (1995). *The winner-take-all society*. New York: The Free Press.
Galenson, D. (2007). *Artists and the market: From Leonardo and Titian to Andy Warhol and Damien Hirst*. NBER Working Paper Series, 13377. Cambridge, MA: National Bureau Economic Research.
Gombrich, E. H. (2006 [1950]). *The story of art* (16th ed.). London: Phaidon Press.
Grabher, G. (2009). Yet another turn? The evolutionary project in economic geography. *Economic Geography, 85*(2), 119–127.
Graw, I. (2008). *Der grosse Preis. Kunst zwischen Markt und Celebrity Kultur*. Freiburg: DuMont.
Greffe, X. (2007). *Artistes et marchés*. Paris: Doc Française.
Hesmondhalgh, D. (2007). *The cultural industries* (2nd ed.). London: Sage.
Hodgson, G. M. (2002). The evolution of institutions: An agenda for future theoretical research. *Constitutional Political Economy, 13*(2), 111–127.
Hodgson, G. M. (2006). What are institutions? *Journal of Economic Issues, XL*(1), 1–25.
Hodgson, G. M. (2009). Agency, institutions, and Darwinism in evolutionary economic geography. *Economic Geography, 85*(2), 167–173.
Illouz, E. (2005, June 2). Berechnung und Hingabe. *Die Zeit, 23*, 62.
International Council of Museums. (2006). *Code of ethics for museums*. Paris: International Council of Museums.
Kaplan, F. (2010, April 10). Showing a couple's eye for art (and money). *The New York Times*. http://www.nytimes.com/2010/04/10/arts/design/10scull.html?_r=0. Accessed 5 January 2013.
Kallir, J. (2007, July 1). The problem with a collector-driven market. *The Art Newspaper, 182*.
Lind, M. (2010, Summer). Laissez faire: Maria Lind on carte blanche. *Artforum, 147*.
Martin, R. (2010). Roepke lecture in economic geography—Rethinking regional path dependence: Beyond lock-in to evolution. *Economic Geography, 86*(1), 1–27.
McCarthy, K. F., Ondaatje, E. H., Brooks, A., & Szántó, A. (2005). *A portrait of the visual arts. Meeting the challenges of a new era*. Santa Monica, CA: RAND Corporation.
Melikian, S. (2009, November 13). Full speed ahead for contemporary works. *The New York Times*.
Menger, P.-M. (1999). Artistic labour markets and careers. *Annual Review Sociology, 25*, 541–574.
Panero, J. (2009, December). The art market explained. *The New Criterion*. http://www.newcriterion.com/articles.cfm/The-art-market-explained-4337. Accessed 15 October 2010.
Pes, J. (2011, June 16). To have and have not. *The Art Newspaper, 7*.
Plattner, S. (1996). *High art down home: An economic ethnography of a local art market*. Chicago: University of Chicago Press.
Plattner, S. (1998). A most ingenious paradox: The market for contemporary fine art. *American Anthropologist, 100*(2), 482–493.
Pollock, L., & Adam, G. (2008, June 5). Why the rise of the private museum is rewriting the rules of the market. *The Art Newspaper*, 1.
Quemin, A. (2006). Globalization and mixing in the visual arts. An empirical survey of 'high culture' and globalization. *International Sociology, 21*(4), 522–550.
Robertson, I. (2005). Art, religion, history, money. In Robertson I. (Ed.), *Understanding international arts markets and management* (pp. 37–61). London: Routledge.
Roelstraete, D. (2010). (Jena Revisited) Ten tentative tenets. *e-Flux Journal, 16*. http://www.e-flux.com/journal/jena-revisited-ten-tentative-tenets/. Accessed 5 July 2010.
Schneiberg, M. (2007). What's on the path? Path dependence, organizational diversity and the problem of institutional change in the US economy, 1900–1950. *Socio-Economic Review, 5*(1), 47–80.
Shiner, L. (2001). *The invention of art*. Chicago: University of Chicago Press.

Sunley, P. (2008). Relational economic geography: A partial understanding or a new paradigm? *Economic Geography, 84*(1), 1–26.

Thornton, S. (2008). In and out of love with Damien Hirst. *The Art Newspaper, 195,* 39.

Vogel, C. (2008, September 15). Damien Hirst's next sensation: Thinking outside the dealer. *The New York Times*. http://www.nytimes.com/2008/09/15/arts/design/15auct.html. Accessed 20 September 2008.

Weil, S. E. (1999). From being about something to being for somebody. *Daedalus,* Summer, 229–258.

White, H. C. (1993). *Careers and creativity*. Oxford: Westview Press.

White, H. C., & White, C. A. (1993 [1965]). *Canvases and careers. Institutional change in the French painting world.* Chicago: University of Chicago Press.

Chapter 5
The Organization and Geography of Making Value

Abstract The third out of the three main chapters, *The Organization and Geography of Making Value*, presents results of a heuristic conceptualization of the selection system of institutions and practices of making value and building careers. The chapter builds on the previous two chapters and pairs the key components of the selection system with concepts and notions from social science disciplines and conceptualizes the competitive process of making value and career building, driven by Western ideals of art, and informed by strategic properties of everyday practices within this heuristic conceptual framework.

Keywords Selection system · Institutions · Practices · Making value · Career building · Heuristic conceptual framework · Competition · Strategic properties

There is general agreement on diagnosing a dominance of the market in the contemporary art world (Boltanski and Chiapello 2005; Graw 2008; McCarthy et al. 2005; Rosler 1997; White and White 1993 [1965]). Although making value for artists and their artworks is based on open competition (Menger 1999) the role of the market can hardly be grasped by conventional economic terms of rational agent, supply and demand, and equilibrium (Greffe 2007; Hutter and Throsby 2008; Plattner 1998; Throsby 2003) or understood separated from its culture (Plattner 1998: 482; Thrift 2000). In fact, the market, here conceptualized as institution, is closely intertwined with two other institutions, discourse and museum, and therefore needs to be viewed within a broader institutional perspective (McCarthy et al. 2005; White and White 1993 [1965]).

Thus, here, the organization and geography of making value of contemporary visual art are conceptualized as selection system of institutions and practices—tentatively called *value making ecology*—that facilitates the competitive process of making value. Central to this conceptualization is a nuanced view on the ideals of creative individualism and autonomy. Autonomy is an ideal that is never fully met; the individual is entangled in their professional world and dependent from other external factors and general conditions. However, a certain degree of autonomy is not ruled out. In other words, creativity and talent are necessary but not sufficient

M. Fasche, *Making Value and Career Building in the Creative Economy*,
SpringerBriefs in Geography, DOI 10.1007/978-3-319-54030-6_5

conditions for enduring value of individual artworks and long stable individual careers; instead creativity and talent need to be valued to eventually be rewarded. This valuation is a continuous but unpredictable process that is socially and spatially entangled, determined by individual practices, power relations, reciprocity and unintended effects, and ultimately resulting in a highly uneven distribution of value or rewards. In other words, the framework of value making ecology aims to provide a heuristic conceptualization of the organizational and spatial complexities of cultural production (Becker 2008 [1982]; Bourdieu 1993; Giuffre 1999; Pike 2009; Pratt 2008; White 1993). In particular, the conceptual framework takes into account not only the social and spatial entanglements but also the strategic properties of everyday practices that produce the outcome of a highly unequal distribution of value or rewards.

5.1 The Selection System—The Heuristic Framework of Value Making Ecology

5.1.1 Value Making Ecology

Here, the very notion of *value making ecology* emerges out of debates about the collective and relational nature of cultural and material production (Giuffre 1999; Pratt 2008; Coe et al. 2008). Value making ecology shifts the focus from "network labor market" (Giuffre 1999: 830), "cultural production chains" (Pratt 2008: 95) and "global production networks" (Coe et al. 2008) to a relational framework that conceptualizes relations as contingent part of institutionalized practices and their strategic properties "to not privilege ties and networks over nodes and agents" (Sunley 2008: 1). The notion of *value* takes into account the growing importance of immaterial qualities such as information, novelty and aesthetic components in the determination of economic value in the rising creative and knowledge economy (Chamberlin 1946 quoted in Callon et al. 2004: 63; Hirsch 1976). It thereby shifts the focus from the production of entities with predetermined value to a processual emphasis on value as continuous variable (Appadurei 1986; Callon et al. 2004) and active constituent in an ongoing dialogue (Thrift 2006: 287) or discourse. The notion of *making* distances itself from an overly productionist perspective by putting forward a more integrated view that includes production, consumption (Grabher et al. 2008) and intermediation in the process of making value. Finally, the notion of *ecology* refers to the organizational diversity of three distinct institutions, market, discourse and museum. The specific day-to-day practices of different stakeholder types of those three institutions intertwine and collectively make value (Becker 2008 [1982]; White and White 1993 [1965]), elsewhere also dubbed art eco-system (Hargreaves McIntyre 2004: 5) or organizational ecology (McCarthy et al. 2005: 1).

Thus, the heuristic framework of value making ecology follows by large the tradition of non-essentialist approaches that put forward a processual emphasis on cultural and material production in terms of collaboration and a complex division of labor at various scales. Yet, rather than analyzing the process primarily in terms of links and interactions between stakeholders and locations value making ecology aims for a more nuanced perspective. It takes the main criticism of relational approaches into account and conceptualizes relations as forms of institutionalized practices and their strategic properties. The main criticisms of relational approaches refer to a selective ontology expressed by overly optimistic associations of networks with collaboration, flexibility, self-organization, autonomy and decentralization, a focus on micro-scale processes, and a rather cursory acknowledgement of the very nature of relationality itself and its manifestation through power relations and actor-specific practices (Sunley 2008: 8).

The heuristic framework integrates selective concepts and notions from sociology of arts, social anthropology, economic geography, old institutional economics, and institutionalist political economy. The framework combines established anthropological and sociological works (Appadurei 1986; Becker 2008 [1982]; Giuffre 1999; White 1993) with analytic strength in emphasizing process and collaboration but which are rather a-spatial in nature with more recent works in economic geography that try to make up for a selective import of an overly positivist ontology of relational approaches from sociology (Lee 2006; Peck 2005; Pike 2009; Pratt 2008; Sunley 2008; Wallerstein 1974). These works are complemented by works from old institutional economics and institutionalist political economy that take into account competition, selection and rewards, and follow the premise that economics cannot be separated from its political and social context (Frank and Cook 1995; Hodgson 2009).

The heuristic framework of value making ecology consists of seven conceptual components. The seven components are unit of value, the three institutions market, discourse and museum, authority, reward scheme, and geography. Each component is paired with respective concepts and notions (Fig. 5.1).

5.1.2 The Unit of Value

The unit of value embodies intangible qualities such as information, novelty and aesthetic component. In contrast to conventional markets where value is determined by absolute terms such as costs of production, marketing and distribution (Hutter and Throsby 2008), value of artists and their artworks relies on a more subjective evaluation of relative performance and rank ordering in a status hierarchy within the art world over time and space (Becker 2008 [1982], Frank and Cook 1995).

Value is made in relation to its professional world, or through associations with other works, another stakeholder, an organization, a venue, or a place. Value becomes visible and is transferred at events such as exhibitions, acquisitions and reviews. Every single event contributes to the artwork's provenance and the artist's

Conceptual components	Concepts and notions
unit of value	the social life of things (Appadurei 1986)
reward scheme	winner-take-all (Frank and Cooke 1995)
market *museum* *discourse*	art world (Becker 2008 [1982]) composite entity (Martin 2010) ubiquity determinism (Hodgson 2009)
authority	intermediary (White 1993)
geography	core and periphery (Wallerstein1974) entangled geographies (Lee 2006) geographical associations (Pike 2009)

Fig. 5.1 The heuristic framework of value making ecology

biography, which may or may not enhance the artist's career and the value of the entire œuvre over time. Only the association with a relatively more valuable brand raises value, or enhances status (Giuffre 1999). In fact, the value of both artist's biography and artwork's provenance, which determine economic rewards, is in flux, continuously revalued in dialogue with and compared to others; in other words, career and provenance, the unit of value, lend themselves to a conceptualization as being processual, also emphasized as the *social life of things* (Appadurei 1986).

5.1.3 Market, Museum, and Discourse

Value is determined in relation to the professional community of the *art world* (Danto 1964; Dickie 1969; Becker 2008 [1982]). The art world appears as an international network of artists, gallerists, collectors, curators and critics and their respective venues such as art studios, commercial galleries, public and private museums, project spaces, art fairs, auction houses and art magazines in ever more places around the world (Becker 2008 [1982]; Rosler 1997). Their joint knowledge of rules and habits of their respective institutions, market, museum and discourse, inform the specific practices and strategic properties of making value (Becker 2008

[1982]; McCarthy et al. 2005; White and White 1993 [1965]). The sum of these individual practices, interrelations, reciprocity and unintended effects determines relative performance and position, or value (Frank and Cook 1995).

Relative performance, ranks and positions, or value, are reflected by status stratification with amateurs ranking at the bottom, professionals in the middle, and superstars at the top of the status hierarchy of the art world (McCarthy et al. 2005). In this sense, the three institutions, market, museum and discourse, not only consist of different types of stakeholders and venues with their respective practices but also of stakeholders and venues of the same type at different status levels; the three institutions are in fact *composite entities* (Martin 2010: 14).

The institutionalized practices of selling and buying, exhibiting, and dialogue strengthen and reinforce the existing institutions of market, museum and discourse of the art world, or the selection system, but they also refine them since stakeholders can be very similar in key aspects but with each type there is some variation due to context or genesis (Hodgson 2009: 169). Moreover, while institutions are not purposeful individuals are. Individuals are self-aware and deliberate and their everyday practices follow strategic intentions but also beliefs and feelings and respond to economic, social, cultural and political circumstances (Hodgson 2009). In other words, institutions and agency are mutually entwined and reinforcing each other through continuing interactions and intentions and desires of individuals, but ultimately institutions are socially constructed (Hodgson 2006). Yet, even though individuals make intentional decisions about their everyday practices of making value the outcome or reward for these practices is unpredictable since status enhancement and value are the net result of the sum of individual practices, power relations, reciprocity and unintended effects (Hodgson 2002). Thus, here, agency is neither free nor predetermined, but caused which is described as *ubiquity determinism* (Hodgson 2009: 171).

5.1.4 Reward Scheme and Authority

The dominance of the market within the selection system manifests through the authority of market stakeholders, like gallerists, in the process of making value and an entrepreneurial reward scheme that is based on open competition.

Gallerists perform an intermediary, gate-keeping, or *authoritative* role in the selection system (White 1993). Based on their aesthetic vision gallerists pre-select artists from a larger pool of talent and make their artworks visible to a wider audience through art shows in the gallery and on art fairs, which may influence what is purchased for public and private collections, what is reviewed in art magazines, blogs and newspapers, and what is picked up for museum exhibitions, shows at other non-profit spaces and for biennales. This rather subtle dimension of power would not exist if agency in the selection system of making value were either uncaused or predetermined (Hodgson 2009: 171). Yet, the level of influence may vary with gallerists ranking in relative higher positions being more influential than those ranking in relative lower positions.

Since art is a positional good (Hirsch 1976), or status good, the entrepreneurial reward scheme takes the form of a *winner-take-all* scheme (Frank and Cook 1995). Positional goods give rise to upwardly pressured competitions for status and value, which are driven by individual and collaborative practices that are informed by both emotion and reason, and whose outcomes are determined by power relations, reciprocity and unintended effects in the art world (Hodgson 2009; Frank and Cook 1995).

According to the winner-take-all reward scheme small differences in relative performance translate into large differences in rewards and value. The nature of this reward scheme resembles a pyramid (Peterson and Simkus 1992 quoted in Alexander 2003: 231) with an enormously wide base, the periphery, leading up to the top, the center, a very small pinnacle of success and stardom (Rosler 1997; Sholette 2005). The pyramid is stratified (Frank and Cook 1995; McCarthy et al. 2005; Plattner 1996; Rosler 1997): at the top of the pyramid are a few superstars who are very well rewarded in terms of status and value. Beyond the superstars are the majority of professionals with many of them struggling to make a living from their practice only. At the bottom of the pyramid is the largest group of stakeholders, the amateurs. The amateurs don't expect to make a living from their practice and remain largely unrecognized and invisible. The result of this highly uneven distribution of value is very different from what individuals may have desired or anticipated in the first place when starting their careers (Frank and Cook 1995).

5.1.5 Geography

Geography in the framework of value making ecology can be conceptualized as *entangled geographies* of both individual places and the interdependence of all places—or in other words territorial and relational geographies (Lee 2006; Massey 1993). Moreover, value is not only made in and across places but also through *geographical associations* with places (Pike 2009).

When following a territorial perspective, individual places reveal concentrations of the different art world stakeholder types belonging to the three institutions of making value (McCarthy et al. 2005). Concentrations can be of more permanent nature made up of different art world organizations and their venues, and stakeholders toiling in them and facilitating events. This would refer to either the scale of a neighborhood or a city. Concentrations can also be of temporary nature bringing together different art world stakeholders for an event at a single venue.

Moreover, each geographical concentration, or scale, is crosscut by a status hierarchy (Plattner 1996: 9), which carries the trajectories of relative performance and ranks of all stakeholders, organizations and their venues while also being in flux. Since making value of artworks and building careers is a reciprocal affair relative performance and position of all stakeholders and their venues are constantly viewed and compared relative to other art world stakeholders and venues over time and space, and manifesting in an unequal distribution of value or rewards.

This is contrary to a conventional understanding of clusters that perceives clusters as being largely internally homogenous (Martin 2010: 14), and doesn't take differences in status into account. In fact, relative higher and relative lower statuses exist in the very same place, or on the same scale. These differences in relative performance and status of stakeholders and venues in the art world can be grasped by *center and periphery* (Wallerstein 1974) on every analytical scale, at single venues, in neighborhoods, cities, regions, nations and globally.

When following a relational perspective all places with permanent or temporary concentrations of different art world stakeholder types of the three institutions of making value are interdependent and compete with each other for status in the same process of making value. In this sense, individual places can be more central or more peripheral relative to other places in the professional world. However, because of the highly unequal distribution of rewards most stakeholders and venues even in most central places are far away from high status and have more in common with their counterparts in other peripheral places (Plattner 1996: 3).

The geographic association with a place confers status to stakeholders, venues and events. Since making value is reciprocal, an association with a place considered of relative higher status may be especially helpful for initial success of promoting new art and starting out on a career. However, the geographic association (where) is part of a wider social process (what, and with whom) of making value. Value is made for individual stakeholders, organizations, and places in relation to its context,

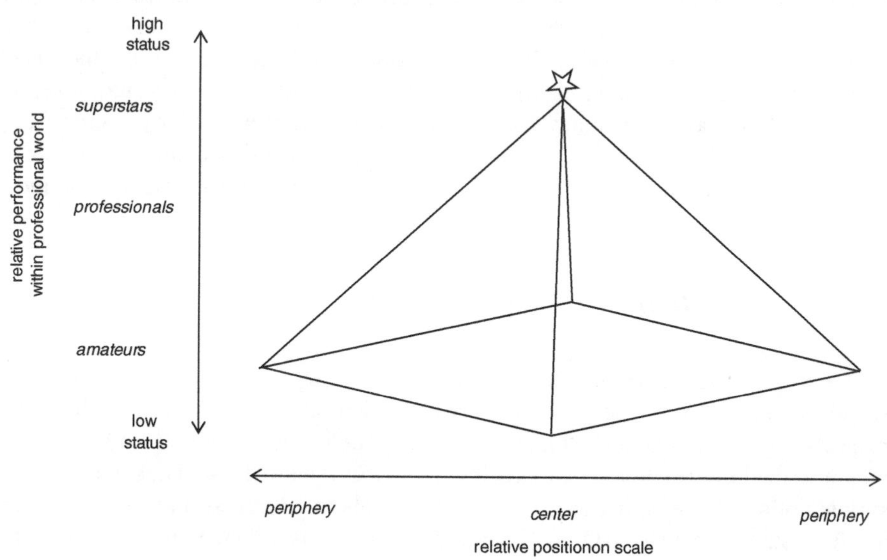

Fig. 5.2 The unequal distribution of value

or its professional world (Becker 2008 [1982]), yet, a world that is not flat but spiky, or unequal, to echo Bourdieu's critical perspective on cultural production (1993).

In other words, relative position on any given scale, either more central or more peripheral, and relative performance in a professional world, either of higher or lower status, are intertwined resulting in an unequal distribution of value with very few stakeholders, organizations and places rewarded with relative high status and relative central positions, and a majority of stakeholders, organizations and places reaping relative lower status and relative peripheral positions (Fig. 5.2). Every more permanent or rather temporary concentration of art world stakeholders on any scale reveals this stylized geography with an unequal distribution of rewards.

5.2 The Competition—Status Desire and Strategic Properties of Making Value

The selection system of a value making ecology sketched above facilitates the process of making value and career building. Value for artists and their artworks is made by specific institutionalized practices, interrelations, reciprocity and unintended effects within the art world over time and space. The process of making value is driven by the enduring success of the Western invention of art as status good (Shiner 2001) and a dynamic of value, price and demand (Veblen 1934 [1899]).

Status desires among both producers and consumers give rise to an upwardly pressured race for status and value. The race manifests in individual relative performance and status levels within the professional world and relative more peripheral or central positions on any given scale, and ultimately results in a highly uneven distribution of rewards (Frank and Cook 1995). In other words, the institutionalized practices of making value are not simply relational, or collaborative, as sometimes emphasized (Sunley 2008) but equally characterized by reciprocate, positional, relative, reflexive, and contingent properties that account for the competitive and enduring nature of the process of making value and career building.

5.2.1 Status Desire

Art as status good emerged in the long 18th century in the Western European societies when art was released from any utilitarian purpose and idealized in terms of art, artist and aesthetics (Shiner 2001). Although value of artists and their artworks is made in relation to an existing art world (Danto 1964; Dickie 1969) the simple notion of something as art evokes the ideals of art, artists and aesthetics and ascribes status or value (Graw 2008). The ideals materialize in the art world institutions and their respective practices such as discourse and dialogue, museums and collecting and exhibiting, and market and selling and purchasing (Shiner 2001). In fact, most art world stakeholders ban economic necessities in an imaginary outside as if art was truly autonomous, if artists were great inventors, and if the quality of art was based on a general theory of perception, but at the same time they engage in the practices of making value and career building following a relational view of art-ness and careers as continuous variables (Graw 2008). This paradox of art, the tension between emotion and beliefs on the one hand, and reason and pragmatism on the other hand, can be seen as the source of the dynamic of making value and career building.

The desire for status, distinction, experience and self-realization but also for income and increasingly for monetary investment and speculative gains attracts artists, gallerists, curators and collectors and other stakeholders to contemporary visual art (Bourdieu 1984; Frank and Cook 1995; McCarthy et al. 2005; Plattner 1998; Veblen 1934 [1899]). The combination of these aspirations and individual wills to make costly investments and incur in considerable economic and social risks to pursue a career in the art world that may or may not be financially well rewarded in the long-term, or to pay significant sums for artworks that may or may not have enduring value, gives rise to an upwardly pressured race for status and value (Frank and Cook 1995). Against the backdrop of an unequal distribution of rewards or value these behaviors appear rationally foolish (Sen 1997) but capture an important human aspect of people following emotions and passions rather than only ratio (Illouz 1997).

5.2.2 *Relationality and Reciprocity*

The provenance of artworks and artists' biographies, and their value, are determined in relation to the professional community of the art world. Gallerists, artists, curators, critics and collectors decide through their cooperative and competitive, or relational, activities and informed by their joint knowledge of doing things how artworks are exhibited, reviewed, sold and collected. Exhibitions, reviews and sales and acquisitions take place, often in seasonal rhythms, in different art world venues including commercial galleries, museums, other non-profit spaces, art fairs, auction houses, biennales, and art magazines (Becker 2008 [1982]; Rosler 1997) and function as positioning and status conferring events that may or may not raise the value for artworks and advance the artist's career.

Conferring status is a reciprocal affair between everyone involved in a particular event at a particular venue in a particular place, and in relation to the rest of the professional community of art world. Stakeholders collectively make value for artists and artworks but by doing so also build their own careers, the reputation of their venues and organizations, and the image of places. Yet, only associations with artworks, stakeholders, venues and places of relative higher status raise the value, advance a career, and build the image of a location.

5.2.3 Relative Performance and Position

For their value artists and their artworks have to be appreciated and compared relative to each other over time and space by the professional community of the art world (Becker 2008 [1982]). Since art is a positional good (Hirsch 1976) relative performance is upwardly pressured to wind up the pyramid from relative lower status to relative higher status and move from a relative peripheral position to a relative more central position on any given scale. Art world events such as exhibitions, reviews and acquisitions position artists and their artworks and confer status that may translate into higher value.

Value is reflected by the artist's biography, the provenance of individual artworks but also the price levels of artworks at galleries and auctions. The artist's biography usually includes the current place of living and working, education, group and solo exhibitions, awards, and artworks in public and private collections. The artwork's provenance refers to exhibitions, reviews and ownerships. Rising price levels at galleries and auctions are commonly associated with higher status or value and a promising art career and stimulate demand and competition among collectors longing for status, distinction, and experience and looking for profitable investments, whereas falling prices signal a loss in status and a declining art career and lower demand (Plattner 1998).

However, more recently the function of price as indicator for value seems increasingly inflated. Naturally, the sum of overall status cannot be increased because every time A rises above B, the only thing changing is who is where in the hierarchy whereas the sum of overall status remains the same (Frank 1985). Although the sum of overall status cannot be increased price levels reflecting different status levels can. In this sense ever-rising price levels and record prices at auctions are primarily an expression of growing competition and speculation due to higher demand and liquidity and collectors' aim to keep-up-with-the-Joneses in the race for value and status (Frank and Cook 1995; Veblen 1934 [1899]). However, record prices and high price levels at auctions may be misleading about value and career development if not sufficiently supported by a biography and provenance consisting of exhibitions, reviews and acquisitions that confer higher status and raise value.

5.2.4 Reflexivity and Contingency

Moreover, only a longer process of relative performance and gradual positioning seems to establish value reflected by provenance and career development, and to stabilize price levels (Frank and Cook 1995; McCarthy et al. 2005).

Contemporary art is contemporary by its very nature. Hence artists and their artworks are in a state of insecurity and speculation about their prospects and value, whether they will be selected, gradually wind up the status pyramid, get well rewarded, and eventually pass the test of time to be integrated into the canon of great artists and great artworks, or whether they remain rather invisible, unrecognized and marginally rewarded or not rewarded at all (Frank and Cook 1995; McCarthy et al. 2005; Roelstraete 2009). In fact, exhibitions, reviews and acquisitions position artists and artworks selected from a larger pool of talent. Of these an even smaller number receives recognition by a wider audience and according rewards, while many equally talented artists remain rather invisible and unacknowledged since higher status and value is limited and highly uneven distributed.

In other words, making value is reflexive as only the cumulation of gradually higher positions in a status hierarchy over time embodied in biography and provenance raise the overall value and advance a career; and contingent since value is not predetermined and as net effect of institutionalized practices, interrelations, reciprocity and unintended effects rather unpredictable.

In sum, value of artworks and artists' careers evolve through a relational framework of a selection system, or a value making ecology, of institutions and practices and their strategic properties over time and space. In fact, practices although shaped by rules and habits of respective institutions can differ significantly. Established rules and habits are applied, varied, converted and recombined or even abandoned for off-path experimentation to fit with individual stakeholder intentions and venues' missions and to respond to developments in and outside the art world such as changing artistic practices, technological innovations, financial pressures, and circles of economic boom and bust (Becker 2008 [1982]; McCarthy et al. 2005; Schneiberg 2007). From this variety of practices new habits may emerge and mature to eventually complement, adjust, twist or even replace habits and rules in the established institutional repertoire. However, each institutional innovation builds on preceding institution instead of accidently appearing out of nowhere (Hodgson 2002; Williamson 1975). Thus, the selections system of institutions and practices, or the heuristic framework of value making ecology, is path dependent revealing a significant degree of continuity and relative stability while evolving incrementally rather than inhering in equilibrium (McCarthy et al. 2005; Shiner 2001; White and White 1993 [1965]).

References

Alexander, V. D. (2003). *Sociology of the arts*. Malden, MA: Blackwell.

Appadurei, A. (1986). *The social life of things: Commodities in cultural perspective*. Cambridge: Cambridge University Press.

Becker, H. S. (2008 [1982]). *Art worlds*. Updated and expanded 25th Anniversary Edition. Los Angeles: University of California Press.

Boltanski, L., & Chiapello E. (2005). *The new spirit of capitalism* (G. Elliott, Trans.). London: Verso.

Bourdieu, P. (1984). *Distinction*. Cambridge, MA: Harvard University Press.

Bourdieu, P. (1993). *The field of cultural production*. New York: Columbia University Press.

Callon, M., Méadel, C., & Rabeharisoa, V. (2004). The economy of qualities. In Amin, A. & Thrift, N. (Eds.), *The Blackwell cultural economy reader* (pp. 58–79). Malden, MA: Blackwell.

Coe, N., Dicken, P., & Hess, M. (2008). Global production networks: Realizing the potential. *Journal of Economic Geography, 8*(3), 271–295.

Danto, A. (1964). The artworld. *Journal of Philosophy, 61,* 571–584.

Dickie, G. (1969). Defining art. *American Philosophical Quarterly, 6*(3), 253–256.

Frank, R. H. (1985). *Choosing the right pond: Human behavior and the quest for status.* New York: Oxford University Press.

Frank, R. H., & Cook, P. J. (1995). *The winner-take-all society*. New York: The Free Press.

Giuffre, K. (1999). Sandpiles of opportunity: Success in the art world. *Social Forces, 77*(3), 815–832.

Grabher, G., Ibert, O., & Flohr, S. (2008). The neglected king: The customer in the new knowledge ecology of innovation. *Economic Geography, 84*(3), 253–280.

Graw, I. (2008). *Der grosse Preis. Kunst zwischen Markt und Celebrity Kultur*. Freiburg: DuMont.

Greffe, X. (2007). *Artistes et marchés*. Paris: Doc Française.

Hargreaves McIntyre, M. (2004). *Taste buds. How to cultivate the art market.* London: Arts Council England.

Hirsch, F. (1976). *The social limits to growth*. London: Routledge & Kegan.

Hodgson, G. M. (2002). The evolution of institutions: An agenda for future theoretical research. *Constitutional Political Economy, 13*(2), 111–127.

Hodgson, G. M. (2006). What are institutions? *Journal of Economic Issues, XL*(1), 1–25.

Hodgson, G. M. (2009). Agency, institutions, and darwinism in evolutionary economic geography. *Economic Geography, 85*(2), 167–173.

Hutter, M., & Throsby, D. (Eds.). (2008). *Beyond price. Value in culture, economics, and the arts*. Cambridge: Cambridge University Press.

Illouz, E. (1997). *Consuming the romantic utopia: Love and the cultural contradictions of capitalism*. Berkeley: University of California Press.

Lee, R. (2006). The ordinary economy: Tangled up in values and geography. *Transactions of the Institute of British Geographers, 31*(4), 413–432.

Martin, R. (2010). Roepke lecture in economic geography—Rethinking regional path dependence: Beyond lock-in to evolution. *Economic Geography, 86*(1), 1–27.

Massey, D. (1993). Power-geometry and a progressive sense of place. In Bird, J., Curtis, B., Putman, T., Robertson, G., & Tickner, L. (Eds.), *Mapping the futures: Local cultures, global change* (pp. 59–69). London: Routledge.

McCarthy, K. F., Ondaatje, E. H., Brooks, A., & Szántó, A. (2005). *A portrait of the visual arts. Meeting the challenges of a new era*. Santa Monica, CA: RAND Corporation.

Menger, P.-M. (1999). Artistic labour markets and careers. *Annual Review Sociology, 25,* 541–574.

Peck, J. (2005). Economic sociologies in space. *Economic Geography, 81*(2), 129–175.

Pike, A. (2009). Geographies of brands and branding. *Progress in Human Geography, 33*(5), 619–645.

Plattner, S. (1996). *High art down home: An economic ethnography of a local art market*. Chicago: University of Chicago Press.

Plattner, S. (1998). A most ingenious paradox: The market for contemporary fine art. *American Anthropologist, 100*(2), 482–493.

Pratt, A. (2008). Cultural commodity chains, cultural clusters, or cultural production chains? *Growth and Change, 39*(1), 95–103.

Roelstraete, D. (2009). What is not contemporary art?: The view from Jena. *e-Flux Journal, 11*. http://www.e-flux.com/journal/what-is-not-contemporary-art-the-view-from-jena/. Accessed 15 April 2010.

Rosler, M. (1997). Money, power, contemporary art—Money, power, and the history of art. *Art Bulletin, LXXIX*, 20–24.

Schneiberg, M. (2007). What's on the path? Path dependence, organizational diversity and the problem of institutional change in the US economy, 1900–1950. *Socio-Economic Review, 5*(1), 47–80.

Sen, A. (1997). Rational fools: A critique of the behavioral foundations of economic theory. *Philosophy & Public Affairs, 6*(4), 317–344.

Shiner, L. (2001). *The invention of art*. Chicago: University of Chicago Press.

Sholette, G. (2005). Heart of darkness. A journey into the dark matter of the art world. In Hall, J. R., Stimson, B., & Becker, L. T. (Ed.), *Visual worlds* (pp. 116–138).New York and London: Routledge.

Sunley, P. (2008). Relational economic geography: A partial understanding or a new paradigm? *Economic Geography, 84*(1), 1–26.

Thrift, N (2000). Pandora's box? Cultural geographies of economies. In Clark, G. L., Feldman, M. P., & Gertler, M. S. (Eds.), *The Oxford handbook of economic geography* (pp. 689–704). Oxford: Oxford University Press,

Thrift, N. (2006). Re-inventing invention: New tendencies in capitalist commodification. *Economy and Society, 35,* 279–306.

Throsby, D. (2003). Determining the value of cultural goods: How much (or how little) does contingent valuation tell us? *Journal of Cultural Economics, 27*(3), 275–285.

Veblen, T. (1934 [1899]). *The theory of the leisure class: An economic study in the evolution of institutions*. New York: Macmillan.

Wallerstein, I. (1974). *The modern world system: Capitalist agriculture and the origins of the European world-economy in the sixteenth century*. New York: Academic Press.

White, H. C. (1993). *Careers and creativity*. Oxford: Westview Press.

White, H. C., & White, C. A. (1993 [1965]). *Canvases and careers. Institutional change in the French painting world.* Chicago: University of Chicago Press.

Williamson, O. E. (1975). *Markets and hierarchy: Analysis and antitrust implications*. New York: Free Press.

Chapter 6
Conclusion

Abstract The *Conclusion* provides a summary of the research approach and the key findings of the case study of making value and career building in contemporary visual art that reveal why rewards are unequally distributed, speculates about a theoretical contribution to an emerging discourse about valuation in economic geography, and sketches potential avenues for future research on making value and career building in the creative economy.

Keywords Creative economy · Making value · Career building · Case study · Contemporary visual art · Unequal rewards · Valuation · Economic geography

This work aims at contributing to a better understanding of how value is made and careers are built in the rising creative and knowledge economy, and why rewards among creative and knowledge workers are unequally distributed. Immaterial qualities such as novelty, design and information have become central for economic growth and prosperity in the rising post-industrial creativity- and knowledge-based economy. Yet, the flip side of the coin reveals that the rise of the creative and knowledge economy seems to be complicit with precarious working conditions, unequal rewards and spatial inequality. This work argues that not only traits conventionally associated with artistic practices and bohemian traditions but also its key logics of value making and career building have permeated into the wider creative and knowledge economy. Thus, studying the logics of making value and career building in one of the arts, here contemporary visual art, may present an opportunity to understand how value is made and careers are built, and why rewards are unequally distributed, or both sides of the same coin, the growth and prosperity perspective and its dark sides, in its possibly purest, or arche-type, form.

This work is explorative, inspired by previous work on location choices of creative businesses and observations within a circle of creative friends and acquaintances, and informed by an upbringing as economic geographer. Expert interviews with 18 gallerists in three cities, New York, Berlin and Los Angeles, about "managing creativity" provided the empirical insight for this work. It was anticipated that managing creativity is primarily determined by its respective local

M. Fasche, *Making Value and Career Building in the Creative Economy*, SpringerBriefs in Geography, DOI 10.1007/978-3-319-54030-6_6

context and that the interviews would reveal differences in practices across places. Yet, the interviewed gallerists seemed to tell the same story between the lines expressed by a constant referencing to other galleries, other locations and a “game”; instead of anticipated differences in practices, the interviewes revealed striking similarities across the three cities. In order to make sense of the findings the empirical analysis was complemented by an intensive study of selected secondary sources and relevant academic literature. The results of this “sense making” are revealed over the course of three main chapters, resulting in a heuristic conceptual framework, tentatively dubbed “value making ecology”.

Analysis of qualitative data from interviews with gallerists about managing creativity revealed motivations and strategies of raising the value of artworks and building artists’ careers and provided initial evidence for the emerging heuristic conceptual framework. Gallerists are passionate about art and strive to promote their aesthetic vision by raising the value of artworks and building artists’ careers. They do so by putting on gallery exhibitions, seeking reviews and inclusion into biennales and museum exhibitions, and placing artworks in public and private collections. Yet, gallerists are constrained by economic necessities to keep their gallery viable, in other words, they are constantly mediating between emotion and reason. Moreover, in order to promote their aesthetic vision by raising values and building careers, gaining knowledge about how to do things seems crucial, especially since there are no entry barriers to open a gallery, having the means to operate a space and calling it a gallery seems sufficient—but only at first sight.

The conceptualization emanates from an economic geography perspective on the organization and geography of the rising creative and knowledge economy that puts forward an emphasis on cultural production as a collective, or relational, process. Hence, empirical findings indicate that making value and career building is not only a collaborative but also a highly competitive process eventually resulting in an unequal distribution of rewards. Analysis of the gallerists’ practices reveals that their activities are not only relational but also reciprocate, relative, positional, reflexive, and contingent. Thus, making value of artworks and building artists’ careers are distinct from conventional value creation of mass produced products. It is no longer tangible and measurable qualities such as costs of production, distribution and marketing with predictable value that stand in the forefront of economic value but rather intangible and subjective qualities such as novelty, aesthetic, and concept, whose value is uncertain. Making value and career building are metonymic and take place in everyday practices of production, intermediation and consumption in urban areas known for their creative scenes rather than in a network of production sites, and follow an open timeframe with unforeseeable outcomes rather than following production schedules. Hence, creativity and talent are necessary but not sufficient conditions for enduring value of individual works and stable long-term individual careers; instead creativity and talent need to be valued to eventually be rewarded in relation to a professional world, ultimately resulting in an unequal distribution of rewards.

A historical-institutional view on making value and career building accounts for the actual stability of institutions that inform practices and strategic properties and puts the invention of new practices and overly positive associations with relationality into a wider historical perspective. It highlights continuities and stabilities as well as shifts and changes in the organization and geography of the selection system of institutions and practices of making value and building careers since the Renaissance and traces how the market evolved as dominant institution.

Since the Renaissance art was slowly elevated into something of higher status and the determination of economic rewards shifted from measurable hence objective means such as hours works to increasingly subjective negotiable means such as novelty and concept, or from absolute performance to relative performance, and from equal to more unequal economic rewards. In fact, the subsequent idealization of art in terms of fine art, artists and aesthetics set the stage for projections and associations and thus art came to inhere in a paradox: art connected to the economy it claims to be distinct from in the first place. Yet, art is not taken entirely over by economic matters, as every notion of something as art evokes the ideals of art and ascribes higher status. This irreconcilable tension between emotion and reason can be seen as the source of the dynamic of making value and career building and has been materializing in the institutions and practices of the selection system of making value and building careers, such as discourse and dialogue, museums and exhibiting and collecting, and market and selling and purchasing.

Gradually the market became the dominant institution within the selection system making possible creative individualism and an open competition, and gallerists emerged as authority in the process of making value and building careers by the end of 19th century. More recently contemporary visual art has grown into a so-called creative industry. The number of artists supplying artworks, collectors buying artworks, gallerists managing creativity, and curators making sense, as well as the number of events where value and career development become visible for the knowledgeable insider have grown globally. The market has become more liquid, price levels have risen and new record prices are frequently set at auction. There seems ever more opportunity to build successful careers in the art world, and desire for status, experience and self-realization motivates individuals to incur in considerable economic and social risks to pursue a career in the art world that may or may not be financially rewarded, or pay significant sums for artworks, that may or may not have enduring value. In fact, the highly visible success of the few may distort perception and blur the fact that the majority of stakeholders are not very well rewarded; and with ever more stakeholders striving for a career in the art world competition for status and rewards is becoming fierce. In other words, stakeholders are no rational actors, but driven by emotion and reason, and stakeholders are intentional by copying, varying, or abandoning practices in the quest to establish. Overall, the selection system of institutions and practices of making value and career building appears rather stable, though not inhering in equilibrium, but changing incrementally through layering, conversion and recombination.

Based on the gallerists' everyday practices and strategic properties and the historical-institutional view of a selection system of institutions and practices this work develops a stylized conceptualization of the organization and geography of institutions and practices of making value and career building, tentatively dubbed value making ecology. To account for competition, selection and the outcome of unequal rewards in the process of making value and career building, this work conceptualizes relations as forms of institutionalized practices and their strategic properties. In doing so, this work shifts the conceptual focus from a relational perspective on cultural production as collective process in terms of links and interactions associated with positive connotations such as collaboration, flexibility and de-centralization, to the very nature of relationality itself that manifests in actor-specific practices, power relations and unequal rewards (Sunley 2008). Due to a perceived scarcity in the conceptual repertoire of economic geography to explain selection, competition and the outcome of unequal rewards, the island of economic geography was left and the author travelled through the archipelago of heterodox economic studies (Peck 2010: 113) by tracing relational and institutional thinking that had been imported into economic geography at an earlier point in time back to their disciplines of origin, sociology, 'old' institutional economics, and institutionalist political economy.

Central to the heuristic conceptual framework are the metonymic relation of work and person, creative individualism in a winner-take-all competition, the determination of quality, meaning and value in relation to a professional world of producers, consumers and intermediaries, and complicity with precarity, and social and spatial inequality. The unequal distribution of value takes the shape of a pyramid on every scale. Value is not only unequally distributed between different places but also within the same place as stakeholders perform relative to each other in the professional world with very few stakeholders rewarded with relative high status and relative central positions, and a majority of stakeholders reaping relative lower status and relative peripheral positions. Since value is unequally distributed, stakeholders in more peripheral positions have more in common with stakeholders in peripheral positions in other places than with more centrally positioned stakeholders in the same place.

In other words, making value and career building is a socially and spatially entangled process with a strong hierarchical but not linear predictable one-directional orientation of cumulating positions within the status hierarchy of a professional world. Value is made and careers are built through associations with relative higher status places, stakeholders, organizations, and works at events within an organizational diverse professional world that is driven by emotion and reason and carries the history of all individual positions while also being in flux and interacting with the wider economic, social, cultural and political sphere. However, with an expansion of the Western centered art world to locations in the former USSR, China, India, Southeast Asia, Gulf region, and South America, it remains to be seen, if Western ideals, and institutions and practices of making value and career building are adopted, blurred, or abandoned in these places.

The heuristic conceptual framework of value making ecology developed in this work may contribute to the emerging debate in economic geography about immaterial qualities such as creativity, novelty and information as central parts in the determination of economic value and individual success in the rising knowledge and creative economy. Research on making value and career building in other professional worlds of the creative and knowledge economy, such as design, film, music, architecture, fashion, literature, and journalism, may try and test the heuristic conceptual framework and may either build upon, refine, or abandon the ontological and conceptual considerations put forward here. Moreover, the composition of the heuristic framework of value making ecology based on concepts and notions from different social science disciplines may indicate a need for closer collaborative endeavor across disciplinary boundaries or the "heterodox archipelago" (Peck 2012: 119) to better understand and conceptualize the organization and geography of value making and career building and the outcome of unequal rewards in the rising knowledge and creative economy.

In addition to trying and testing, building upon, refining, or abandoning the heuristic conceptual framework of value making ecology developed in this work, three major research avenues may lend themselves for future work on making value and building careers in the rising creative and knowledge economy: First, how do gender, race, ethnicity, and geographical origin shape the process of making value and building careers? Second, what is the role of government and public policy in the process of making value and building careers? And third, with growing concerns about economic and spatial inequalities how could a vision of a good city (Amin 2006) or just city (Fainstein 2011) be realized?

References

Amin, A. (2006). The good city. *Urban Studies, 43*(5–6), 1009–1023.

Fainstein, S. S. (2011). *The just city*. Ithaca, NY: Cornell University Press.

Peck, J. (2012). Economic geography: Island life. *Dialogues in Human Geography, 2*(2), 113–133.

Sunley, P. (2008). Relational economic geography: A partial understanding or a new paradigm? *Economic Geography, 84*(1), 1–26.

Chapter 7
Epilogue

Abstract The *Epilogue* sketches the main characteristics of the art market bust in the wake of the 2008 financial crisis and the subsequent market recovery. The *Epilogue* briefly reflects on the market contraction and shift in focus from over-valued living artists at auction to critical reflection and dialogue about artworks facilitated by commercial gallerists, refers to mixed fortunes brought by a market recovery, and a recent rise of prices levels for living artists at auction.

Keywords Art market · Contemporary visual art · Auction · Commercial gallerists · Bust · Price · Value · Recession · Recovery

During the months following the Lehman Brothers crash, economies on both sides of the Atlantic went bust, governments bailed out banks, people lost jobs and investments, and austerity policies were implemented. At the same time consumer confidence dropped sharply and the art market contracted (McAndrew 2011). Sales at galleries and on art fairs slowed down, fewer amounts of money were spent at auctions and U.S. museums lost at least 20% of the value of their endowments (Gerlis 2008; Kaufman 2009; Vogel 2008). The reduced liquidity in the art market confirmed that the longest boom cycle in just about one century of modern art market history had ended.

Only two years after the bust the market showed signs of recovery (McAndrew 2011). Consumer confidence returned and both auction houses and galleries made respectable results again (Szántó 2011). After dropping by 66% during the downturn in 2009 the value of sales rose again to levels just above those of 2006 before the height of the boom (McAndrew 2011: 101) and "the numbers" rebounded. In December 2009 gallerists had reported that 500,000 were the new million at Art Basel Miami Beach, one of the most prestigious art fairs (Adam et al. 2009: 1), one year later the trend had reversed with 100,000 being the new 40,000 (Adam et al. 2010b)—signaling that the market was back (Taylor 2010). Yet, the pace of doing business had been seemingly slower and attitudes had become more intellectual with dialogues about art at galleries and on art fairs and less uncritical bidding at auction (Adam et al. 2010a; Melikian 2011).

M. Fasche, *Making Value and Career Building in the Creative Economy*,
SpringerBriefs in Geography, DOI 10.1007/978-3-319-54030-6_7

Yet, the recovery of the art market brought "mixed fortunes" (McAndrew 2013). Collectors predominately purchased either artwork by established artists at the top or young emerging artists at the bottom of the market while demand for artwork by middle tier artists had been recovering more slowly (Adam et al. 2010a; Burns 2013; McAndrew 2011). If anything, the gap between average values of sales at the top and the middle widened during the recovery (Burns 2013). At the same time the art world has continued to expand. The number of events and venues where artworks are shown to the public has continued to grow. Worldwide more than 100 biennials can be counted (Lowry 2012: 130), the number of art fairs has grown from 65 in 2005 to 189 in 2011 (Adam 2012), and numerous museum projects are underway such as the Guggenheim Abu Dhabi, new museums in China and several private collector museums worldwide (Adam 2013). Moreover large Western galleries have expanded their gallery spaces locally and opened gallery braches overseas, especially in Hong Kong and mainland China (Adam 2012) while new young galleries emerged and started to thrive "back home", especially if the gallerist had worked for an established gallery before "going solo" (Pollock 2011).

Meanwhile recent maximum results at auctions have reached pre-recession heights (Rice 2012). In November 2012 Jeff Koons's "Tulips" sold for US$33.7 million at Christie's New York to an anonymous bidder raising the previous auction record for the artist at auction (Melikian 2012). Yet, the title of the most expensive living artist is no longer held by Jeff Koons. In October 2012 Gerhard Richter's "Abstraktes Bild (809–4)" previously belonging to Eric Clapton, sold at Sotheby's London for US$34.2 million, or more than 30 times of what Eric Clapton had paid for it in 2001 (Reyburn 2012), to an anonymous bidder. The price level for Richters has been seemingly increasing since a recent traveling retrospective exhibition that was shown at Tate Modern in London, Centre Pompidou in Paris, and the Neue Nationalgalerie in Berlin (Vogel 2012a). But not all artists have been affected by the market recovery in the same way; for example, the market for artworks by Damien Hirst currently shows deflation. Hirsts acquired during the market boom between 2005 and 2009 have only been resold with an average loss of 30% value in price, while, in fact 1700 Hirsts offered at auction since 2009 have failed to sell altogether (Rice 2012).

Still, in fact, overall results at the top end of the market have never been better (Adam 2012). During the Fall Auctions in November 2012 collectors spent nearly US $1 billion at Sotheby's and Christie's New York on "tried-and-true" artists (Vogel 2012b). Both auction houses were reported to have achieved their highest total ever in their respective histories (Melikian 2012; Vogel 2012a, c). And some people in the art world have started to wonder about a new bubble, they say maximum price levels seem to be too high, distorted, even irrational (Thibaut 2012: 28).

References

Adam, G. (2012, June). Fair or foul: More art fairs and bigger brand galleries, but is the model sustainable? *The Art Newspaper, 236.* http://old.theartnewspaper.com/articles/Fair-or-foul-more-art-fairs-and-bigger-brand-galleries-but-is-the-model-sustainable/26672. Accessed 20 June 2012.

Adam, G. (2013, January). What's in store for the market? *The Art Newspaper, 242.*

Adam, G., Burns, C., Harris, G., & Mason, B. S. (2009, December 5–6). The going is tough: But stronger sales at all levels than last year. *The Art Newspaper, 1.*

Adam, G., Burns, C., Pollock, L., & Ruiz, C. (2010a, June 16). Art Basel's most wanted: Established artists. *The Art Newspaper*, 1.

Adam, G., Burns, C., Gerlis, M., & Katz, M. M. (2010b, December 4–5). Who needs celebrities? It's the serious collectors that count. *The Art Newspaper*, 2.

Burns, C. (2013, March). While the rich get richer .... *The Art Newspaper, 244.* http://old.theartnewspaper.com/articles/While-the-rich-get-richer/28991. Accessed 4 March 2013.

Gerlis, M. (2008, November). "Hot" categories cool rapidly as crisis bites. *The Art Newspaper, 196*, 61.

Kaufman, J. E. (2009, January). Museums make deep cuts in face of global financial crisis. US budgets slashed, programming reduced and expansions halted. *The Art Newspaper, 198.*

Lowry, G. (2012). Battle of the biennials. *The Economist—The World in 2013,* 130–131.

McAndrew, C. (2011). *The global art market in 2010. Crisis and recovery.* HD Helvoirt: The European Fine Art Foundation (TEFAF).

McAndrew, C. (2013. March 14). US retakes top spot in art sales from China. *The Art Newspaper.*

Melikian, S. (2011, November 4). Uptown from wall street, a bull market. *The New York Times.* http://www.nytimes.com/2011/11/05/arts/05iht-MELIKIAN05.html. Accessed 5 November 2011.

Melikian, S. (2012, November 16). Investors fly to contemporary art. *The New York Times.* http://www.nytimes.com/2012/11/17/arts/17iht-melikian17.html?_r=0. Accessed 17 November 2012.

Pollock, L. (2011, January). Alive and kicking despite the slump. *The Art Newspaper, 220.*

Reyburn, S. (2012, October 13). Clapton's Richter fetches $34 Million, 30 times purchase. *Bloomberg Businessweek.*

Rice, A. (2012, November 21). Damien Hirst: Jumping the shark. *Bloomberg Businessweek.*

Szántó, A. (2011, May 23). The season that was. http://www.artworldsalon.com. Accessed 23 May 2011.

Taylor, K. (2010, December 3). Blues skies and blues-chip sales at Art Basel Miami. *The New York Times.* http://www.nytimes.com/2010/12/04/arts/design/04artbasel.html. Accessed 5 December 2010.

Thibaut, M. (2012, November 17). Die Einheizer. *Der Tagesspiegel, 28.*

Vogel, C. (2008, November 16). In faltering economy, auction houses crash back to earth. *The New York Times.* http://www.nytimes.com/2008/11/17/arts/design/17auct.html. Accessed 18 November 2008.

Vogel, C. (2012a, November 13). $375.1 million art sale is Sotheby's record. *The New York Times.* http://www.nytimes.com/2012/11/14/arts/design/contemporary-art-sale-is-sothebys-record.html. Accessed 14 November 2012.

Vogel, C. (2012b, November 15). Warhol paintings of Mao tops auction at Philipps. *The New York Times.* http://www.nytimes.com/2012/11/16/arts/design/warhol-painting-of-mao-tops-auction-at-phillips.html. Accessed 17 November 2012.

Vogel, C. (2012c, November 14). Relentless bidding, and record prices, for contemporary art at Christie's auction. *The New York Times.* http://www.nytimes.com/2012/11/15/arts/design/record-breaking-prices-at-christies-auction.html. Accessed 15 November 2012.

Chapter 8
Making Of

Abstract The *Making Of* provides insight into the methodology of this work by revisiting the research process of qualitative data analysis and building theory from cases. The *Making Of* reveals how this work was inspired by observing highly unequal economic rewards among creatives in Berlin, how these initial observations were put into the wider discourse of a rising creative economy in post-industrial societies, how expert interviews with commercial gallerists in three cities revealed strategic properties of everyday practices of making value and building careers, and how a stylized heuristic conceptualization of a selection system of institutions and practices of making value and career building came gradually into being.

Keywords Case study · Theory building · Qualitative data analysis · Heuristic concept · Selection system · Institutions · Practices · Strategic properties · Making value · Career building

This work is largely phenomenon-driven and its methodological approach was initially inspired by grounded theory but ultimately followed a script of "qualitative data analysis" (Seidel 1998) to "build theory from cases" (Eisenhardt and Graebner 2007). Based on analysis of qualitative data from three different case study sites, complimentary secondary sources, and relevant academic literature both the research focus of this work and the ontology of an emerging heuristic conceptualization of the organization and geography of making value of contemporary visual art were gradually refined. The research process consisted of five successive though in fact interrelated and overlapping research phases whose respective findings were turned into the individual chapters of this work.

These five phases included discursive framing, fieldwork, empirical analysis, literature study, and conceptualization. The findings are represented in seven chapters. Chapters 2 and 6, and 1 and 7 provide the discursive framing of this work, while the three main Chaps. 3, 4 and 5 reveal the results of empirical analysis, literature study, and the development of a heuristic conceptualization. The research process of this work was carried out as iterative, progressive and recursive cycling between empirical evidence, secondary sources, relevant literature, and the emerging

M. Fasche, *Making Value and Career Building in the Creative Economy*,
SpringerBriefs in Geography, DOI 10.1007/978-3-319-54030-6_8

heuristic conceptual framework rather than a linear research process of completing one research phase after the other (Seidel 1998).

8.1 Discursive Framing

Discursive framing was predominately performed ex post the main research process of fieldwork, empirical analysis, literature study, and conceptualization. This work was originally motivated by intrinsic interest and curiosity about creative workers and their everyday practices to establish or become successful, and informed by preceding research on the relation between places undergoing urban regeneration, or gentrification, and location choices of creative business services. This earlier work reveals that the habitus of the location embodied in the location image, amenities and the presence and activities of creative people matters more than spatial proximity to suppliers or customers (Fasche 2006; Fasche and Braun 2007) as suggested by studies on conventional industry clusters. Furthermore, this work was inspired by my day-to-day observations in a gentrifying neighborhood I was living in at the time and a wider social circle of creative people I was hanging out with in Berlin. Designers, visual artists, filmmakers, curators, and other creative types were doing cool projects but not making much if any money. Just maybe one or two were doing very well financially. In addition, while helping out in a commercial gallery of a befriended gallerist for a short period of time I observed intriguing practices such as refusing to sell to certain collectors and selling out shows before they had even opened to the public. These observations nurtured the idea of selecting contemporary visual art from the roster of so-called cultural or creative industries as case study for this work.

After the fieldwork, the case study analysis, and developing the heuristic conceptualization, I recalled these initial observations and choice to position my findings in the wider context of a rising knowledge and creative economy, and to sketch avenues for future research. Relevant literature in my home discipline and adjacent fields of study was selected to reflect these initial observations and frame this work. During the research process it had become evident that a case study from the arts may reveal the logics underlying the process of how value is created and how careers are built in the rising knowledge and creative economy in its possibly purest form and thus help to better understand why economic rewards are unequally distributed among creative and knowledge workers (*Introduction,* Chap. 2). By evaluating the main findings of this work, speculating about potential contributions, and sketching avenues for future research this work came to completion for the time being (*Conclusion*, Chap. 6). To distinguish between the test of time, required to establishing value of artworks and building long stable careers, and speculative short-term value, brief descriptions of the contemporary history of the art market were added. These historial snapshots highlight how the largely self-regulating selection system of institutions and practices of making value and building careers is dominated by the market and its cycles of market boom (*Prologue*, Chap. 1) and bust (*Epilogue*, Chap. 7).

8.2 Fieldwork

The fieldwork was explorative and focused on commercial gallerists as intermediaries between artists and collectors and their everyday practices of "managing creativity" in different urban contexts. Three different case study sites were selected, Berlin as a "new happening place for arts and culture", New York as the "established arts and culture capital", and Los Angeles as a "bourgeoning place for arts and culture". The fieldwork was guided by the observations mentioned above and framed by the assumption about the importance of place in an increasingly networked world, and the growing challenge of mediating between art for art's sake and economic subsistence. From the perspective of an academic upbringing as an economic geographer I intuitively anticipated that "managing creativity" was primarily determined by its respective local context, and thus, that the fieldwork would reveal differences in practices across these places.

Qualitative data was collected in expert interviews with a total of 18 commercial gallerists, five in Berlin, five in Los Angeles and eight in New York between January and September 2007. A total of 40 gallerists were approached for an interview, six in Berlin, seven in Los Angeles and 27 in New York. The sole selection criterion was a diverse geography of gallery locations across the sub-sample within each city. The potential interviewees were selected from credible preselections, i.e. the line-up of the Art LA, "The New Los Angeles International Contemporary Art Fair", that had taken place just weeks before the fieldwork (artfairs, inc. 2007), a list of superstar galleries listed in an academic paper on galleries in Chelsea (Halle and Tiso 2005: 59), and a list of gallery locations produced as part of a consultant study on cultural and creative industries in Berlin (Fasche and Mundelius 2008: 110). Later on, potential interviewees in New York were selected by visiting different gallery quarters such as Chelsea, Lower East Side, DUMBO and Williamsburg. Four interviews—two in Berlin, one in New York and one in Los Angeles—were arranged through personal contacts and recommendations.

Initially, the potential interviewees were contacted via email with a brief personal introduction and description of the interview purpose. While contact and arrangement of an interview via email worked well in Los Angeles, it neither did in New York nor in Berlin. According to advice from David Halle, who has been studying galleries extensively, I changed the way of approaching from emailing to walking into the galleries, trying to meet in person to arrange an interview for another day. This direct method was successful when I was able to meet the gallery owner in person. In bigger New York galleries with front desk gate-keeping "gallerinas" (Hoffman 2008) I was politely told to send an email with my interview request to the gallery but I hardly ever received any replies.

Thus, the sample is biased towards smaller galleries with fewer employees where it was possible to meet the gallery owner in person when visiting the gallery (Baxter and Eyles 1997).

The length of the interviews varied significantly between 20 and 80 min but on average the interviews took 40 min. All interviews were conducted in person, 16 in the back offices of the galleries and two in nearby cafés. All but one interview were recorded and transcribed verbatim. One gallerist refused to be recorded and therefore notes were taken instead. Eleven interviews were conducted in English, while the other seven were conducted in German as the mother tongue of two interviewees, one in Los Angeles and one in New York, was German. All interviewees were guaranteed that quotations from the interviews would not be attributed to individual interviewees.

The interviews were semi-structured and followed a guide of broader themes but allowed space for other topics and dialogues to emerge (Schoenberger 1991: 182). The guide of themes included the history of the gallery, the professional background and vision of the gallerist, the gallery program and artists' stable, the collectors, collaboration, the role of the location and the city, the role of internet and art fairs, recent changes in the art world, and future projects. After eighteen interviews a saturation point seemed to be reached (Baxter and Eyles 1997). With every interview it had become more evident to me that despite the diverse locations within cities and different national and regional contexts I was told the same story between the lines expressed by a constant referencing to other galleries, other locations, and "a game". Instead of intuitively anticipated differences between the three places I had found striking similarities, but, at the time, I had neither an explanation nor a conceptual language for it.

8.3 Empirical Analysis, Literature Study, and Conceptualization

In order to make sense of the empirical findings, use a conceptual language and identify a theoretical gap in the economic geography literature to potentially contribute to, the empirical analysis was complemented by an intensive study of selected secondary sources and relevant academic literature.

The intensive study of secondary sources refers to a constant following of articles and publications by selected long-term observers of the art market. These include primarily articles in the weekly The Art Newspaper, the art market's main trade paper (Velthuis 2011: 191), and in dailies of the three respective cities, The New York Times, The Los Angeles Times, and Der Tagesspiegel, as well as reports by The European Fine Art Foundation (TEFAF), the international art dealer association Confédération Internationale des Négociants en Oeuvre d'Art (CINOA), the think-tank The Rand Corporation, and Artprice, a self-acclaimed world leader in art market information.

The intensive study of academic literature refers to two main bodies of research and three interrelated contemporary debates, here listed with their main, though subjectively selected, voices. The first body of literature consists of works engaging with the organization and location of cultural production more generally (Bourdieu 1993; Grabher 2002; Hesmondhalgh 2007; Hirsch 2000; Peterson and Anand 2004; Power and Scott 2004; Pratt 2011) and contemporary visual art in particular (Becker 2008 [1982]; Giuffre 1999; Graw 2008; Moulin 1994; Plattner 1996, 1998; Quemin 2006; Rosler 2010; White 1993; White and White 1993 [1965]). The second body of literature refers to works reflecting on relevant theoretical paradigms, concepts and notions such as relationality (Bathelt and Glückler 2003; Sunley 2008; Yeung 2005), institutions (Hodgson 2002, 2006; Veblen 1934 [1899]), evolution (Martin 2010; Schneiberg 2007), production (Pratt 2008; Reimer 2009), and competition and selection (Frank and Cooke 1995).

The recent debates include three discourses. The first and most relevant debate for this work is the emerging conceptual discourse on valuation, quality and meaning as integral parts of the production process in the creative and knowledge economy, and market making (Barthelt and Glueckler 2011; Beckert and Aspers 2011; Berndt and Boeckler 2009; Callon et al. 2004; Lee 2006; Participants of Economic Geography 2010 Workshop 2011; Pike 2009). The second relevant debate refers to the discourse that conceptualizes places and networks as co-developing beyond a global-local dichotomy (Alderson and Beckfield 2004; Allen 2010; Castells 1996; Peck 2005; Sassen 1991). The third relevant debate frames this work, namely a more general discourse on changing institutions and practices underlying a new quality of capitalism and its processes of territorialization, and urban and regional development (Boltanski and Chiapello 2005; Florida 2002; Hay 2013; Scott 2008).

Empirical analysis, literature study, and conceptualization were closely interrelated during the research process of this work. The research process followed a rigorous practice of iterative, progressive and recursive cycling among qualitative data, secondary sources, relevant literature, and the emerging conceptual framework (Eisenhardt and Graebner 2007; Seidel 1998). The character of this cycling was nomothetic in order to develop a stylized conceptualization of making value and career building and thus at times brushed over idiosyncrasies of local and national contexts (Clark 1998; Schoenberger 1991: 183).

Each cycle consisted of the analytic steps of noticing, collecting and thinking which in fact happened rather simultaneously since when you notice you already collect and think (Seidel 1998: 2). "Noticing" included making observations in the material and coding them. "Collecting" meant sorting these codes and relating them to each other. "Thinking" referred to trying to make sense of the assembled codes and their relations by recognizing patterns. However, while "thinking" new discoveries were made and holes in the emerging conceptual framework were "noticed". This initiated a new cycle of making observations in the material, coding, collecting, sorting, and making sense only to identify another conceptual hole in the emerging conceptualization initiating a next cycle and so on and so forth—accompanied by the sometimes rhetorical, sometimes worryingly but frequently asked question "are we there yet?" (Grabher and Stark 2009).

During this process of iterative, progressive and recursive cycling both research focus and the ontology of the emerging heuristic conceptual framework were gradually refined and the underlying premise materialized. The notion of gallerists "managing creativity" as intermediaries between artists and collectors was refined to intentionally aiming to "make value" by raising the value of artworks and building artists' careers while in a reciprocate manner building their own careers. Moreover, the gallerists' everyday activities of making value (Orlikowski 2002) may have been anticipated as independent entrepreneurial practices but they are in fact closely socially and spatially entangled with the value making activities of other stakeholders in a wider selection system of institutions and practices—in which the gallerists play a dominant role as authority. Yet, it became apparent that making value and career building is not just a collective networked endeavor with other stakeholders but also a highly competitive process, a winner-take-all competition, with outcomes of highly unequally distributed rewards. Place, or geography, plays a key role in the process of making value and career building albeit not alone but together with the professional world, or organization. Place offers access to events of the professional world and the opportunity of associations with the particular place, its venue, and other stakeholders that may or may not enhance the value of artworks and build a career. At the same time each place itself is a relative position in a wider network of competing places. With respect to an observed mounting challenge of mediating between art for art's sake and economic subsistence it became evident that it is in fact the irreconcilable tension between the two ideals, emotion and reason, that informs and drives the institutions and practices of making value and career building.

Taken together, the analytic focus of gallerists "managing creativity" in different urban contexts shifted to the organization and geography of a competitive process of "making value" with gallerists performing a role of authority within a wider selection system of institutions and practices. Moreover, the underlying premise materialized, proposing that "creativity and talent are necessary but not sufficient conditions for enduring value of artworks and long stable careers, instead creativity and talent need to be valued to eventually be rewarded".

During this process of gradual refinement the strategic properties of everyday practices of making value, the components and corresponding notions and concepts of a selection system of institutions and practices were gradually revealed—though at times it felt like "performing ballet on a bed of ontological quicksand" (Pudup 1998: 384 quoted in James 2012). After very many cycles of observing, coding, collecting, sorting, and making sense the strategic properties of making value (*Practices of Making Value-Evidence form Gallerists*, Chap. 3), the components of a selection system of institutions and practices (*A Historical-Institutional View on Making Value*, Chap. 4), and their pairing with corresponding notions and concepts could eventually be integrated within a heuristic conceptual framework of a selection system of institutions and practices—dubbed tentatively as value making ecology—that facilitates the competitive process of making value and career building (*The Organization and Geography of Making Value*, Chap. 5).

References

Alderson, A. S., & Beckfield, J. (2004). Power and position in the world city system. *American Journal of Sociology, 109*(4), 811–851.

Allen, J. (2010). Powerful city networks: More than connections, less than domination and control. *Urban Studies, 47*(13), 2895–2911.

artfairs, inc. (2007). *art la. The New Los Angeles international contemporary art fair.* Los Angeles: artfairs, inc.

Bathelt, H., & Glückler, J. (2011). *The relational economy: Geographies of knowing and learning*. Oxford: Oxford University Press.

Bathelt, H., & Glückler, J. (2003). Toward a relational economic geography. *Journal of Economic Geography, 3*(2), 117–144.

Baxter, J., & Eyles, J. (1997). Evaluating qualitative research in social geography: Establishing 'rigor' in interview analysis. *Transactions of the Institute of British Geographers, 22*(4), 505–525.

Becker, H. S. (2008 [1982]). *Art worlds*. Updated and expanded 25th Anniversary Edition. Los Angeles: University of California Press.

Beckert, J., & Aspers, P. (2011). Value in markets. In Beckert, J., & Aspers, P. (Eds.), *The worth of goods. Valuation and pricing in the economy* (pp. 3–40). Oxford: Oxford University Press.

Berndt, C., & Boeckler, M. (2009). Geographies of circulation and exchange: construction of markets. *Progress in Human Geography, 33*(4), 535–551.

Boltanski, L., & Chiapello, E. (2005). *The new spirit of capitalism* (G. Elliott, Trans.). London: Verso.

Bourdieu, P. (1993). *The field of cultural production*. New York: Columbia University Press.

Callon, M., Méadel, C., & Rabeharisoa, V. (2004). The economy of qualities. In Amin, A., & Thrift, N. (Eds.), *The Blackwell cultural economy reader* (pp. 58–79). Malden, MA: Blackwell.

Castells, M. (1996). *The rise of the network society*. Oxford, Malden MA: Blackwell.

Clark, G. L. (1998). Stylized facts and close dialogue: Methodology in economic geography. *Annals of the Association of American Geographers, 88*(1), 73–87.

Eisenhardt, K. M., & Graebner, M. E. (2007). Theory building from cases: Opportunities and challenges. *Academy of Management Journal, 50*(1), 25–32.

Fasche, M., & Mundelius, M. (2008). *Kreativ Wirtschaften. Kreativwirtschaft in Berlin am Beispiel von Friedrichshain-Kreuzberg*. Berlin: Aperçu:

Fasche, M., & Braun, B. (2007). "We are newtowners"—Place matters. Habitus, creative business services and gentrification in inner Sydney. In Dose, G., & Kuhlenbeck B. (Eds.), *Australia—Making space meaningful* (pp. 139–151). Tuebingen: Stauffenburg.

Fasche, M. (2006). Creative people and gentrification: "Sowing the Seeds of Demise?" Evidence from Newtown, Sydney. *ERDKUNDE, 2,* 147–156.

Florida, R. (2002). *The rise of the creative class*. New York: Basic Books.

Frank, R. H., & Cook, P. J. (1995). *The winner-take-all society*. New York: The Free Press.

Giuffre, K. (1999). Sandpiles of opportunity: Success in the art world. *Social Forces, 77*(3), 815–832.

Grabher, G. (2002). Cool projects, boring institutions: Temporary collaboration in social context. *Regional Studies, 36*(3), 205–214.

Grabher, G., & Stark, D. (2009). Commentary. Frequently asked questions. *Environment and Planning A, 41*(2), 255–257.

Graw, I. (2008). *Der grosse Preis. Kunst zwischen Markt und Celebrity Kultur*. Freiburg: DuMont.

Halle, D., & Tiso, E. (2005). Lessons from Chelsea. A study in contemporary art. *International Journal of the Humanities, 3*(11), 45–66.

Hay, I. (Ed.). (2013). *Geographies of the super-rich*. Cheltenham: Edward Elgar.

Hesmondhalgh, D. (2007). *The cultural industries* (2nd ed.). London and Los Angeles: Sage.

Hirsch, P. M. (2000). Cultural industries revisited. *Organization Science, 11*(3), 356–361.

Hodgson, G. M. (2002). The evolution of institutions: An agenda for future theoretical research. *Constitutional Political Economy, 13*(2), 111–127.
Hodgson, G. M. (2006). What are institutions? *Journal of Economic Issues*, *XL*(1), 1–25.
Hoffman, J. (2008, March 30). Gatekeepers to the art world. *The New York Times*. http://www.nytimes.com/2008/03/30/fashion/30gallerinas.html. Accessed June 02, 2008.
James, N. (2012, January 31). Re: Deleuze and all that. *Crit-GEOG-FORUM(at)JiscMail.ac.uk.*. https://www.jiscmail.ac.uk/cgi-bin/webadmin?A2=ind1201&L=crit-geog-forum&P=R65338&1=crit-geog-forum&9=A&I=-3&J=on&d=No+Match%3BMatch%3BMatches&z=4. Accessed March 18, 2013.
Lee, R. (2006). The ordinary economy: Tangled up in values and geography. *Transactions of the Institute of British Geographers, 31*(4), 413–432.
Martin, R. (2010). Roepke lecture in economic geography—Rethinking regional path dependence: Beyond lock-in to evolution. *Economic Geography, 86*(1), 1–27.
Moulin, R. (1994). The construction of art values. *International Sociology, 9*(1), 5–12.
Orlikowski, W. J. (2002). Knowing in practice: Enacting a collective capability in distributed organizing. *Organization Science, 13*(3), 249–273.
Participants in the Economic Geography 2010 Workshop. (2011). Editorial. Emerging themes in economic geography: Outcomes of the economic geography 2010 workshop. *Economic Geography, 87*(2), 111–126.
Peterson, R. A., & Anand, N. (2004). The production of culture perspective. *Annual Review of Sociology, 30,* 311–334.
Peck, J. (2005). Economic sociologies in space. *Economic Geography, 81*(2), 129–175.
Pike, A. (2009). Geographies of brands and branding. *Progress in Human Geography, 33*(5), 619–645.
Plattner, S. (1998). A most ingenious paradox: The market for contemporary fine art. *American Anthropologist, 100*(2), 482–493.
Plattner, S. (1996). *High art down home: An economic ethnography of a local art market.* Chicago: University of Chicago Press.
Power, D., & Scott, A. J. (Eds.). (2004). *Cultural industries and the production of culture.* London: Routledge.
Pratt, A. (2011). *An economic geography of the cultural industries.* In Leyshon, A., McDowell, L., & Lee, R. (Eds.), *The SAGE compendium of economic geography* (pp. 323–337). London: Sage.
Pratt, A. (2008). Cultural commodity chains, cultural clusters, or cultural production chains? *Growth and Change, 39*(1), 95–103.
Quemin, A. (2006). Globalization and mixing in the visual arts. An empirical survey of 'high culture' and globalization. *International Sociology, 21*(4), 522–550.
Reimer, S. (2009). Geographies of production II: Fashion, creativity and fragmented labor. *Progress in Human Geography, 33*(1), 65–73.
Rosler, M. (2010). Culture class: Art, creativity, urbanism. *Hermes Lecture*. AS' s-Hertogenbosch: Hermes Lecture Foundation.
Sassen, S. (1991). *The global city: New York, London, Tokyo.* Princeton (N.J.): Princeton University Press.
Schneiberg, M. (2007). What's on the path? Path dependence, organizational diversity and the problem of institutional change in the US economy, 1900–1950. *Socio-Economic Review, 5*(1), 47–80.
Schoenberger, E. (1991). The corporate interview as research method in economic geography. *Professional Geographer, 43*(2), 180–189.
Scott, A. J. (2008). *Social economy of the metropolis: Cognitive-cultural capitalism and the global resurgence of cities.* Oxford: Oxford University Press.
Seidel, J. V. (1998). Qualitative data analysis. http://www.qualisresearch.com/DownLoads/qda.pdf. (originally published as Appendix E: Qualitative data analysis. In Seidel, J. V. (1998), *The Ethnograph v5.0: A Users Guide.* Colorado Springs, CO: Qualis Research).

Sunley, P. (2008). Relational economic geography: A partial understanding or a New Paradigm? *Economic Geography, 84*(1), 1–26.

Veblen, T. (1934 [1899]). *The theory of the leisure class: An economic study in the evolution of institutions*. New York: Macmillan.

Velthuis, O. (2011). Damien's dangerous idea: Valuing contemporary art at auction. In Beckert, J., & Aspers, P. (Eds.), *The worth of goods. Valuation and pricing in the economy* (pp. 178–200). Oxford: Oxford University Press.

White, H. C. (1993). *Careers and creativity*. Oxford: Westview Press.

White, H. C., & White, C. A. (1993 [1965]). *Canvases and careers. Institutional change in the French painting world.* Chicago: University of Chicago Press.

Yeung, H. W.-C. (2005). Rethinking relational economic geography. *Transactions of the Institute of British Geographers, 30*(1), 37–51.

Appendix

List of Interviewed Commercial Gallerists

Joe Amrhein, Pierogi Gallery, New York (Williamsburg) and Leipzig (Spinnerei)
Kim Foster, Kim Foster Gallery, New York (Chelsea)
François Ghebaly, Chung King Project, Los Angeles (Chung King Road)
Todd Hosfelt, Hosfelt Gallery, New York (Hell's Kitchen) and San Francisco (South of Market)
Gloria Kennedy, Gloria Kennedy Gallery, New York (DUMBO)
Nancy Margolis, Nancy Margolis Gallery, New York (Chelsea)
Ulrich Mueller, Ulrich Mueller Berlin and Architektur Galerie Werkraum, Berlin (Torstrasse and Karl-Marx Allee)
Mihai Nicodim, Kontainer Gallery and Chung King Project, Los Angeles (Chung King Road)
Patrick Painter, Patrick Painter Inc., Los Angeles (Bergamot Station)
James Rojas, Gallery 727, Los Angeles (Downtown)
Marisa Sage, Like The Spice Gallery, New York (Williamsburg)
Nelja Stump, Galerie Tristesse deluxe, Berlin (Karl-Marx-Allee)
Werner Tammen, Galerie Tammen, Berlin (Checkpoint Charlie)
Andrea Teschke, Friedrich Petzel Gallery, New York (Chelsea)
Susanne Vielmetter, Susanne Vielmetter Los Angeles Projects and Berlin Projects, Los Angeles (Culver City) and Berlin (Holzmarktstrasse)
Cai Wagner, Galerie Herrman Wagner, Berlin (Scheunenviertel)
Jan Wentrup, Galerie Jan Wentrup, Berlin (Torstrasse)
Andre Zarre, Andre Zarre Gallery, New York (Chelsea)

M. Fasche, *Making Value and Career Building in the Creative Economy*, SpringerBriefs in Geography, DOI 10.1007/978-3-319-54030-6

FSC
www.fsc.org
MIX
Papier | Fördert
gute Waldnutzung
FSC® C083411

Kolibri 360 GmbH
Ferdinand-Jühlke-Straße 7
99095 Erfurt, Deutschland
produktsicherheit@kolibri360.de